Perceptual Intelligence

by

Tom Lane

authorHOUSE®

AuthorHouse™
1663 Liberty Drive, Suite 200
Bloomington, IN 47403
www.authorhouse.com
Phone: 1-800-839-8640

© 2008 Tom Lane. All rights reserved.

No part of this book may be reproduced, stored in a retrieval system, or transmitted by any means without the written permission of the author.

First published by AuthorHouse   4/9/2008

ISBN: 978-1-4343-5949-0 (sc)

Printed in the United States of America
Bloomington, Indiana

This book is printed on acid-free paper.

To all the people who danced with me on this journey

FOREWORD

I WROTE THIS BOOK because many years ago, I had an experience that showed me that I valued "knowing" someone more that I valued the actual person. I had been confronted at a workshop about "who I really was" and after a great struggle, I admitted that I did not know who the "real" me was since I spent most of my time trying to uphold an image of who I thought I should be. It was an enormous weight off my shoulders to come clean at that moment and just show up without a mask on. A few nights later, at a Halloween party (how appropriate!), when my friends took off their costume masks, I saw that they wore an image mask that I had never noticed before. I was stunned. I realized at that moment that I never truly looked at anyone, since I was mainly concerned about maintaining my own mask.

It took me a few years and some very powerful experiences to really grasp what I was glimpsing on that night. In my life, I had lost my Perceptual Intelligence in favor of my Conceptual Intelligence. We all lose sight of the people and the world around us when we begin to know them. Knowledge paints a picture or an image that overlays the actual experience of the other. Whether that other is a spouse, a child, a co-worker, or even a stranger on the street. And the greatest loss is the inability to see our own being, in our quest to "know thyself". Knowledge about, is not the actual event or person. It is simple as that.

This is written for all those people who wish to regain the direct experience of the world and the people around them. It is a putting of our living back into its rightful sequence of "looking before we know".

It is a challenge to the way we have become accustomed to living our lives. It is about having "fresh eyes" to again experience the newness of each and every moment. If you go down this path, be prepared to step outside your identity and your attachments. If you decide to live in this actual world rather than the conceived one in your head, then by all means, read on. Tom Lane

THIS BOOK IS BEYOND THINKING

PERCEPTUAL INTELLIGENCE is the intelligence of awareness, a natural intelligence that all human beings possess that is outside the realm of thought. It is not magical, mystical, supernatural, or otherwise special, except to the world of normal thought based intelligence. And there is the rub. We believe that anything beyond what our conceptual mind can grasp, belongs to some other worldly entity or the borderline crazy set. This is not any of that. It is right in front of you.

There is a wonderful story in Zen called the empty boat that captures what this book is about. If you are out on a river rowing a boat along and you see an empty boat drifting toward you, you would probably just row your boat out of the way. Very simple. But if you were in the same situation and the boat is coming toward you with a person in it, you may instead call out to the person to watch where they are going or to get out of your way. In the first situation, we simply see and adjust, but in the second, we bring our ideas into play. Who has the right of way, who was here first, and what are the rules of the waterway. The first was seeing and acting. The second was seeing, thinking, analyzing, judging, verbalizing and then maybe acting. What this says, is that we have made living very complicated when we immediately use our thinking mind to make the world more complex and difficult than it needs to be. We have come to believe that this amazing tool called thinking is our highest form of being. I see that insertion of our thinking into every aspect of how we experience life to be at the core of most of the suffering and sorrow in the human condition. This book is beyond thinking, and in some ways, a returning to the natural awareness that is key to our peace of mind, and ultimately key to our very survival. And since it is beyond thinking, it may be difficult at times to see what the book is pointing to. It is not a new idea, it is beyond thought.

PERCEPTUAL INTELLIGENCE

WHAT IS INTELLIGENCE? Have you ever wondered what that means? How would you answer that? For me, it all has to do with conceptual thinking. And that is a very restrictive and limiting way of defining intelligence.

The way we usually relate to the world around us is through our conceptual frameworks. Ideas, concepts, beliefs, values and knowledge are acquired consciously and unconsciously, throughout our childhood and adult lives. Intelligence then, is considered to be the ability to retain the knowledge contained in this framework, and to have an excellent memory for facts, quotes, formulas, as well as an ability to use them in solving problems or "thinking." Intelligence also pertains to knowledge about oneself and others. We commonly understand "knowing oneself" as knowing our values, "real" beliefs, history and past conditioning.

I refer to this framework as Conceptual Intelligence (CI). It dominates our everyday life and relationships. It is very useful in the physical world of making things, going somewhere, or doing simple work. However, it is not the only kind of intelligence. There is another kind that I believe is much more powerful. I call it Perceptual Intelligence (PI).

Where CI has to do with our active thought processes, PI is concerned with out passive observation processes. Since it is passive, it has been generally dismissed as a minor function of human intelligence. We have been so conditioned to our active conceptual side that we have abandoned any serious effort to enhance and expand our perceptual side. Our preoccupation with CI leads to many difficulties, since we so often mistake our idea about something as the thing itself. For example, I am not a concept; you are not a concept; life is not a concept; relationships are not concepts; and love is not a concept. Yet we have concepts *about* all of these, and that is the problem. We have overridden our ability to simply observe with perceptual intelligence, with conceptual intelligence. That is living backwards: percept should always lead concept. The concrete experience should always lead its abstracted form. See before you believe.

All valid new understandings have come through a simple process of observation, and then conceptualization. This is how we teach children about the world. We point at a dog (which the child is observing directly) and say "dog" (the concept). The legend tells us that Sir Isaac Newton sat under an apple tree and observed the effect of gravity before he devised the formula for its behavior. Albert Einstein posed mental image problems to observe, and then conceptualized his theory of relativity. Always, the breakthroughs come first with observation, and then with conceptualization. Somewhere along the way, many of us reverse this order and become lost in our thoughts. We let our concepts dominate our percepts and become perceptually blind.

Our relationships with the world, with others, and even with ourselves become purely conceptual. We no longer see other human beings as they are. We now see them as Germans, Asians, Conservatives, Jew, or as beautiful, ugly, and the like. Stereotypes, whether positive or negative, with their built-in judgments, now determine what we see and how we should react. We have even dismissed the word "perception" when we say to others, "that is just your perception" when what we actually mean is that is how your THINK about it, not perceive it.

When does this happen in our growth process? I am not sure, but I do know that by the time I was 21, I was experiencing myself mostly as a concept. I had my values, beliefs, images, identities, and opinions all firmly in place that defined who I was. I no longer had contact with me as an alive and aware human being, directly in touch with my environment. Worse, I did not know that there was any other way to be. I was hooked into the world of concepts. Concepts ruled my life. Breaking the concept habit was extremely difficult and painful; without them I thought I would surely die.

Now I realize that there was a certain truth to that belief. For when I began to let go of the images and concepts of me, my identity died, as did my illusion of self. The notion of me as some separate and historical being also died – and a human being was born.

Perceptual Intelligence (PI) opens our eyes to "see" more clearly the world around us. I have found that there are two arenas in which this sight is developed, the first is process awareness. Here, PI is the ability to watch how relationships unfold over time: how the interaction between things or people evolve, without our judging or defending how that is happening. PI requires a discipline of focus, that is, the ability to pay close attention to something over a prolonged period *without intervening in any way*, mentally or physically. I think of the enormous PI of the early astronomers who would patiently and painstakingly observe the skies year after year to map the stars and the paths of the planets.

The second arena of PI is that of "seeing" connections, what some call "systemic" or "space-oriented" capability. PI in this sense observes the multiple connections occurring simultaneously. It sees how things fit together and align with each other. It sees how a change in one part leads to shifts in other parts or areas. Again, we see this system without judgment or desire to fix, but only to gain deep understanding. While the process seeing happens over what we call time, the system seeing happens in a more space oriented or wholistic fashion. The combining of these two ways of seeing is sometimes called "cosmic consciousness."

Increasing our ability to practice these two arenas of PI underlies everything in this book. Paradoxically, words are the tools of Conceptual Intelligence (CI), not PI, which, though it may not be mute, cannot be expressed in words. A Zen saying illustrates this paradox. "Don't look at my finger when I am pointing at the moon." Our tendency is to look at the words (the finger) and not what the words are pointing to (the moon). Our PI must be direct, not through the concepts conveyed by words.

In our efforts to learn what PI is, or wanting to become practicioneers of PI, or even resisting it and wanting to refuse it, we are still dominated by CI. When we find ourselves doing these things, our practice is just to observe what we are doing. That is PI. We must always remember that there is nothing we can do, or path we can follow, to achieve PI. Any path or "how to" is just more conceptual baggage that will have to be discarded sooner or later. PI lightens the load of concepts; and just casts the light of the eye on what is emerging. That is why it is called enlightenment.

CONTRASTING PERCEPTUAL AND CONCEPTUAL INTELLIGENCE

ONCE, AFTER RIDING MY MOTORCYLE, I compared the difference between what I was doing and driving a car. In both cases all the rules of the road apply, but to survive on a motorcycle requires a more persistent level of awareness than that required for safely operating an automobile. You need a heightened sense of where you are in the traffic, how visible you are to trucks and cars, what are the road conditions – gravel, drains, potholes – that signal danger, and how to escape close calls. This kind of defensive driving required on a motorcycle is an example of Perceptual Intelligence (PI). One can sit through classes on precautionary practices, but if awareness of the here and now is not sustained while actually on the bike, PI gives way to CI, greatly increasing the chances of catastrophe. One knows the ideas, but lacks the capability to respond immediately to the clear and present danger. Clarity of conscious attention is a hallmark of PI.

What specifically differentiates these intelligences?

1. With PI, we are aware of how things unfold over time. We watch as things develop and change to form patterns of interaction. This could be between a person and a machine, or between two persons, or group to group, or even patterns of our own behavior. With PI, no judgment is involved in watching the unfolding. In contrast, CI is concerned with ends

and conclusions. We ask, where is this leading? Is it good? Is it wrong? CI wants answers and results and judgments.

2   PI is tuned into the connections between various aspects of a multifaceted whole. We notice relationships between parts, and of parts to the whole. PI is systemic, ecological. CI is interested in developing a history and body of knowledge surrounding a certain part or episode of the whole. CI appeals to specialists, experts, and accumulators of knowledge. It is analytical and functional.

3   PI enhances clarity and focus so that we may perceive directly the movement of all aspects of living. CI is concerned with the abstractions derived form direct perception that are captured in words depicting particular versions of reality.

4   PI can only be exercised in the present; it has nothing to do with the past events or future possibilities. CI, on the other hand, is always either concerned with memory, or projections into the future, or attempts to predict events or outcomes.

5   PI deals with simple, observable facts that are beyond debate. Dialogue is the method of exploring the implications of these facts. (Socratic dialogue is probably the best-known example). CI focuses on the duality of all conceptual positions, since verbalized thought is always dualistic. CI debates the rightness or goodness of various abstracted conclusions. It operates in the realm of ethics and morality.

6   PI is heightened sensory capability. It emanates from the quietness of the mind that expands to include things like intuition, compassion, joy, and feelings of peace and love. CI is concerned with sets of values and beliefs handed down from one's social, cultural, or familial history. Some of these may be extracted from PI, but more often they are taught as stand-alone laws or "truths." CI tends to be authority-based and is often used to control the behavior of others.

CI dominates the mental activity of most people. It can so overwhelm us that we totally lose all PI. This loss causes what is referred to as "someone living in his or her own world." The degree to which we are dominated by CI is the degree to which we create destructive and dysfunctional systems, cultures, and individuals.

It is <u>impossible</u> to enhance the PI through more and more CI effort. This attempt is the trap of following any guru or authority or system that promises higher consciousness or spiritual development. PI is entirely a personal experience. Abstractions and concepts (such as this book) can only point out that there is something else, but must always fall short of delivering the "real thing." Looking for PI outside the self is a vain search.

These are the facts about PI that have shifted my living in relationship to the various human beings I have encountered along my way. Some of these facts will disturb the "common knowledge" that comprises our collective CI. As you feel that disturbance, simply watch where it takes you, without expressing any emotion. Do not deny or accept the disturbance. Do not give yourself over to the reaction. Observe it and see that this is the playing out of your unique humanness, then see what happens.

SUMMARY

<u>Perceptual Intelligence</u>
- Process Awareness
- System Awareness
- Real Time Sensing Presence
- Facts Commonly Observed

- Dialogue for Understanding
- Consciousness

<u>Conceptual Intelligence</u>
- Knowledge/Outcomes
- Fragmented Rightness
- Abstracting from the Actual
- Opinions and Historical Conditioning
- Debate over Positions
- Cleverness

OUR PERCEPTUAL INTELLIGENCE CONNECTION

EVEN THOUGH FEW PEOPLE LIVE in PI, we all have this within us. And it is always trying to break through to affect our experience. A large proportion of the population has reported having some sort of what is called psychic experiences. Anything from strong deja vu, to esp, to some sort of premonition, or to something as simple as a strong hunch or gut feeling about something. I think this is our PI breaking into our experience at moments when the conceptual barrier is a little relaxed.

I remember a very powerful experience years ago while driving from Cleveland to Columbus Ohio. It was a weekend evening with lots of traffic on the interstate. As I was driving, I noticed a wonderful sunset in the western sky and as I drove I slowed down a bit so I could glimpse the changing colors. As I topped a hill, there was an accident ahead and the traffic was halted in both lanes. I easily slowed down, but as I pulled up to the last car, a strong voice in my head said "pull off the road"! At first I resisted, but it repeated the message and I pulled my car onto the shoulder of the highway. The next car over the hill was going very fast as he topped the same hill, slammed on his brakes and slid sideways past me to within 6 inches of the bumper of the car I would have stopped behind. I sat there frozen, wondering why I was the only car on the shoulder and how I should have been rear ended by that next car. It really gave me pause.

Years later, I now understand that it was that quieting of my thinking mind by looking at the sunset that allowed my PI "knowing" to come to me and protect me. I have heard many similar stories in my life from all kinds of people. What we tend to do is write it off as just coincidence or luck. This is what the CI based mind wants us to do since this is entirely out of its control.

There have been many studies trying to prove or disprove this phenomena and they always are inconclusive. The reason is that perceptual intelligence can not be controlled by conceptual intelligence. To set up an experiment is a conceptual endeavor. It sets parameters, measures, methods, and some hypothesis to be proven. This activity is a way to actually increase the boundary that blocks our PI capability. Increasing the blockage is not a good way to discover if this is real or not. The more stringent the experiment, the less we are apt to deliver. To the CI mind, this "proves" that this is some sort of imagination. They can not see that the dynamic of the whole process is part of the problem. CI blinds us that way.

But, make no mistake, that this other PI "knowing" (I do not like using that word, but it seems to fit) is always with us. Next time you have one of those "paranormal" experiences, do not try to explain it, justify it, capture it, or anything else. Just observe it and stay with it as long as you can. See what it shows you.

CI CAN NOT USE PI

AS YOU BEGIN TO GRASP the amazing power of PI, one of the normal responses is to begin to figure out how to use this power to further my own success, position, fame or fortune. I have heard people say, "If this is real, then tell me who is going to win the next horse race so I can lay a bet on it". Forget it, it can not be done. Our thinking mind can not use the PI as some kind of tool or method for any personal gain. The very notion of doing that, is a resistance to experiencing PI.

As I mentioned before, experiments conducted in the realm of CI can never prove or disprove the existence of PI. But, I did come across a woman, several years ago, who told me a fascinating story. She was part of a group of "psychics" in Russia who were part of an experiment by the military to see if they could use these paranormal powers to spy on enemies of the state. (I recently heard that the US conducted similar studies) The experiment was a little different than most lab type experiments in that they were given total freedom to enhance their abilities in any way they saw fit. She said most did meditation and other mind clearing type of exercises. After a while, she said that several of them were capable of doing "remote viewing". This means that they could observe something happening in some distant location while sitting quietly in a room. They consistently reported being able to see and hear what was going on. The spying implications were, of course, monumental.

But, here was the catch. When they were told to use this power to observe anything that would give some advantage to the military, the power DISAPPEARED! The people in charge of the experiment were baffled, as were the participants, since most of them were not adverse to spying on enemies. But the power of PI would not go there. CI can not control PI for its own ends.

So, at this point, you may be asking what is the point of this then. And there is no point in terms of the CI world. This is to show us how the CI world works by stepping out of it. It shows the limitations of the thinking world. It shows how we have lost our natural way for the normal way. It reminds us that our calling is to be free of the bounds of conditional thought and "see" the beauty of the world.

THE FUNCTIONING OF PERCEPTUAL INTELLIGENCE

PI PROCESS AWARENESS

EVERYTHING IS A PROCESS. The trouble is, that we do not see that since we are mostly coming at the world from our knowledge base. The process is simply the unfolding of events, steps, activities, behaviors, or other sequences. It is how things get made, information is transferred, travel is accomplished, and absolutely anything you can imagine. It all is a process. Now, most people tend to ignore the process in favor of looking for the outcomes of the process or the content and meaning. The outcomes are our CI judgments of the goodness or badness of what we call the end result.

Of course, there is no such thing as an end result. This is a good test of your process seeing right now. Why is it the truth that there is no end result of any process? Take some examples and play with them in your head. Think of the process of cooking dinner. Is it an end when the dinner is completed? Or just a shift in the process from cooking to eating? Processes shift all the time, but they never end.

There is nothing fancy about process, nor is there anything good or bad about process. It just is. And this is key to being able to see process. We must do it non-judgmentally. All judgments come out of our CI history of how we have calculated good and bad, right and wrong. We are very quick to jump to our judgmental conclusions about any processes we encounter. This is the problem, we make decisions without sufficient data about the process. When that happens, we can create more problems and disruptions than we solve. This is about "looking before you leap" or observing before deciding. Old simple wisdom that is rarely practiced.

In my teaching of this in my work to help transform organizations, one of the dilemmas was that managers would learn the word "process" and miss the actual. They thought that I was teaching a new concept for manufacturing and consistently missed the point. Our CI always wants to know. It wants to capture some idea and put it into it's storehouse of knowledge. This proved to be a very big problem for me, since as I kept wanting to show people how to "see" process, what they heard was me beating on an idea that they already understood. It is not and idea. PI has no ideas in it, it only has the actual observation of process or system. Ideas come later after clarity of the process is gathered.

And this is the paradox of writing this book. I am using the tools of CI (words) to point to something that has no words and can not be known, but is the most valuable thing you can possess. Your awareness shows you the world you live in. There is no other way of directly experiencing it. Instead, most of us, by the time we have grown, only experience the world through the filter of our past knowledge. We live in a worded world of CI and have lost our way.

LEVELS OF PROCESS AWARENESS/THINKING

PROBABLY THE BIGGEST PRACTICAL APPLICATION of PI process was that which began the shift in the world of manufacturing. It was the simple notion of moving from "making things" to "managing a process that makes things". This simple but profound new awareness was a turning point in how people worked to produce goods because it allowed the use of tools like Statistical Process Control to manage quality to levels unheard of in traditional factories. The problem is that we have not pursued strongly enough the extension of this notion to higher levels of process management.

As I see it, there are 4 levels of process that need to be managed. The first is the simple physical level where we have witnessed a revolution already. This means the actual material we are working with and the machines that work on the material. The second level of process is the level of information. This means the way information moves to and with the physical product. This area has some attention to it and we are now looking at the process of measuring, scheduling, standardizing, planning, etc. This body of data surrounds the physical product and allows the physical process to move in the appropriate manner. This is changing and will continue to change as the physical level demands more timely and accurate information. This is PI at its most simple level.

The next level of process is the behavioral/communication process that is uniquely human, and uses the information and to manage the physical process of making things. Here we are less clear since the level of complexity just took a big jump. That is due to the fact that each human being brings a fairly unique set of behaviors and communication skills to the situation. On top of that, we have the collective behavior (called the culture) that is always unique to a specific location or factory. Managing the process of behavior and communication must be a self-managed affair. We have tried the authoritarian approach over the years and it can have some effectiveness over short periods of time, but ultimately, each and every player in the operation must self manage their own behavior and act and communicate effectively. That means sharing essential information to the parties who need it, supporting the next physical process and the prior physical process, asking questions to reveal breakdowns in physical and informational processes, reinforcing the notion of managing process instead of simply demanding outcomes, tracking planning processes to insure that top down direction is translated effectively into actions and tasks, etc. All this behavioral process is driven by the final level to manage, and that is the thinking process.

Thought process drives behavior process drives information process drives physical process. How we think always creates what we make and do. Most people have been conditioned to work and think a certain way by years of experience in factories and in society in general. This certain way is not "one" certain way, but often in a variety of ways. This makes this task very monumental. Their old way of thinking is the process by which people make sense of the world they live in, tends to be automatic and unconscious. Everyone has it and very few could describe how it works within them. (I remember confronting an excellent plant manager with the idea that "yes you are really good, but you don't know why you are good because you don't really know how you think about this" He protested and I asked him to tell me how he thinks, not what he thinks. He stammered and finally gave in and it was a beginning of a beautiful friendship)

So here is our paradox. Physical process is an outcome of a thought process that drives a behavior process that drives an information process that creates the physical process. The easiest process to alter is the physical process and the hardest process to alter is the mental process. But as we alter the physical process we come in conflict with the information process that is misaligned, and the behavior process that is also misaligned. These processes must be changed, but they are there as extensions of the mental process that is behind all of it! Back we go to the most difficult part of the problem. But to think, why don't we just start with the mental process in the first place is to set yourself up for failure. There are few people who can work on this level, so we painstakingly work from the physical to the information to the behavior to the mental. And if this wasn't hard enough, it all takes place in a dynamic and ever changing system, which is made up of numerous inter-related processes in the outside environment. All of this is set up to sustain the status quo and resist change. But it does happen and it can happen.

So in the most practical of situations, we can see the need for developing our Perceptual Intelligence capability to see process. Practicing on the simple physical level gets us used to just observing process without judgment. Moving up to more difficult processes becomes an obvious next step. Of course, this can be done anywhere, not only in some factory. It can be observing your household chores, your ways of passing information and behaving as a family or social group, and as always, the thought process never goes away. It is always there to be observed.

PI SYSTEM SEEING

EVERYTHING IS A SYSTEM. If you remember, back a few pages ago, I said everything is a process and now everything is a system. And the answer is "yes". When you observe the world as a movement, everything is a process. When you observe the world as a wholistic snapshot, then everything is a system. A system means that everything is connected and in some symbiotic kind of support relationship. The support I am describing here is neither good nor bad, right nor wrong, healthy or unhealthy. It is just a fact that any thing you focus on will have an elaborate support structure surrounding it in order to maintain its existance. This is true if you are looking at your own life, a community, a part in a factory, your car, your house, your family, your nation or whatever. Nothing exists without a system of support surrounding it. Most of us never notice the system around us until it breaks down.

I used to use the example of the simple task of cooking a hamburger in a exercise to help people appreciate system support. I would have them brainstorm all the things that are necessary for this simple task to be done correctly. They would come up with 20-30 things in just a few moments and it was always a little bit startling for them. They took time to consider how much stuff has to be in place to do such a simple task. Because we lack PI system awareness, we never notice all that is constantly going on around us. And we do not have to notice all if it, but when you set out to change something or improve something, you better take into consideration the systemic supports.

Whenever a system has been in place for any length of time, the various support elements become complimentary (more on this later) which means that there is a give and take exchange going on that sustains the current way of operating. Whether that is your car, your family, your self, your company or anything else. This exchange becomes invisible to us over time and we pretty much take it for granted. It is like the first time a young person goes out on their own and is shocked at all the stuff that is necessary to set up a household. Look around you right now and see all the things that are sustaining your existence right now.

Because we lack this systemic PI, we begin to think we are stand alone individuals. We think it is every person for themselves in this world. We sincerely begin to believe that we can do it by ourself. We lose sight of the way we are part of and creator of the culture and society that surrounds us. We forget that how and what we think and do has cause and effect and cause reactions in an ever going circular dynamic. We forget that we are the world and it is not something "out there" to fight against.

A word of caution as you may begin to look around at the system you live in. It can be very overwhelming to take it in all at once, expecially, if you have any need to control. The system is there and it is happening, you do not have to control it, fix it, hide from it, or anything else. Just be aware that there are many, many factors going on and we can learn to flow with them, see how they affect us, how we affect them, and just how it all works. With that understanding, you may find opportunities that you never saw before.

MORE PI SYSTEM SEEING

HOW DIFFERENT DOES THE WORLD LOOK through the eyes of the aware PI viewer? Not very different. What really is different is how we experience ourselves in that world. This Zen saying captures it perfectly. "Before enlightenment, trees are trees and clouds are clouds, after enlightenment, trees are trees and clouds are clouds." The trees and the sky look the same, but who we are *with them* changes significantly.

Viewed through CI, we see the world as created by others or by nature, and take little or no responsibility for it. It is simply an object, to which we react. If we see something as beautiful, we're pleased; if something appears ugly, we're displeased or disgusted. We're disconnected onlookers, watching the world like we watch a movie. There is a strong separation between us and what's being projected on the screen. We feel no sense of choice regarding how that "reality" out there can be experienced. It's just there: the world "makes us feel" one way or another.

On the other hand, through a PI, systems view, we see both the constant interplay between what is going on "out there," and what is going on in our minds, as the formation of reality. What the world means is a mental operation. That constant interplay between what's going on and the meanings we assign it, are inseparable. PI system-based thinkers always know that we are choosing to see the world and interact with it in a particular way. In other words, we are actively engaged in creating our world.

This creation is not primarily physical, even though we may make material things out of our imaginations. Rather, conceptual creation assigns meaning to things. One who looks at things with PI knows that conceptual meaning making, is a tool to create, manage and understand physical things, while a CI-based view is that somehow the "meaning of things" is inherent in the things being observed. I suspect this is why so many CI-based thinkers spend great amounts of time and energy trying to determine what is intrinsically good and bad, right and wrong, beautiful and ugly.

The CI-based view is derived from the physical sciences, where it can be useful to determine what is hard and soft, hot and cold, etc. These physical properties are inherent in things at the physical level of thinking, and can be useful for making things or doing physical work. The difficulties begin when we transpose that thinking to higher life forms.

PI awareness sees that concepts, and the words that express them, are simply tools to be utilized. So mere words can never cause a reaction in a person with PI awareness. In a CI-based view, on the other hand, concepts rule, because to CI-based persons, words are experienced as reality, thus causing an endless stream of "good" and "bad" reactions. CI-based persons cannot see that the "reality" and their reactions are self-created. No others out there make them feel the way they do. Money illustrates this point. CI-based thinkers believe there is inherent worth in money. They really believe that gold or precious stones or dollars have intrinsic worth, or that they impute worth to their owners. That is why these people crave "wealth" of this kind. They cannot see that money or precious metals are valuable only because society has conceptually treated them so. If we were all to change our minds about them, dollars and gold would be worthless. They would just be paper and stones.

So what is the use of this understanding, that we create meanings? First, it will help us redirect our energy from trying to fix the external world, to looking inward and reconstructing our process of conceptual creation. We may thereby stop constantly reacting to words, and begin simply to see what is happening. From there we may be able to use conceptual tools to discover ways to improve what needs improving.

Second, this understanding may help us save the energy we currently waste on judging things and people. This energy can then be redirected toward understanding and discovering the common bond connecting all people.

Finally, it will allow natural change and growth to take place in our being. For CI-based thinkers, growth stops, because they make themselves a concept, i.e. professional, father, mother, macho, sensitive, boss, American, etc., and attach themselves to that concept. Such concepts are usually referred to as one's "identity." The attachment to concept is an attachment to non-life, because it is fixed and unchanging, whereas everything in the living system is dynamic and changing. Concepts are non-living tools, whose only use is as tools. A rock by a stream is more alive than the greatest concept, since at a subatomic level, particles are dancing and mutating endlessly. But thoughts have no life of their own. The human being is alive and the thinking process is part of their living, it is a movement of energy. But the words that are generated are not alive, they are marks on the paper or noise in the air. When we mistake ourselves for the thought we have of ourselves, then we have stopped all growth and have entered a realm of non-life. The tool of thought is not alive in itself.

The Perceptually Intelligent understand that conceptual tools are a means to describe the dynamics of growing and living systems, including themselves. They never mistake the concept or its verbalized form for the reality of life in its happening

RINGS OF SYSTEM SEEING

AS WITH PROCESS LEVELS, system seeing has somthing similar to levels, only I would better describe them as rings. These would be similar to the rings of a bullseye. At the center, we have a point of focus, then a sequence of rings emanating outward to form bigger and bigger circles. A simple exericise to see this is to look around you at this moment. See the all that surrounds you in an immediate fashion. Then pop up out of yourself and see you sitting in your house (or other structure) and notice this level of surrounding support. Then, pop up another level to see the neighborhood in which your house is located, then up to the communitiy, then the region, and so on. Each of these levels provides some kind of support to your very existance at this moment. Some of the support is very direct and immediate and some of it is indirect and very subtle. All of it is connected to you sitting here, right now, reading these words.

Most of us are unaware and really do not need to be aware of these elaborate rings of system support constantly surrounding us. And, in most situations, if we are encountering a problem in our world, we can adjust the immediate factors in the first ring to gain a solution. But as problems get more complex, we can find solutions only in the more removed rings. Say you are feeling cold, so the most immediate solution is to go to the thermostat and turn up the heat. Problem solved. But what if there is a storm outside and the power line is down to your house. Now the solution is on an extended ring (outside the house). Or suppose that the a transforming station has been knocked out and the whole neighborhood is without power, then the ring is wider. And what if the power generation plant has been shut down because of a malfunction. The ring gets bigger and as you can see, the problem gets larger and more complex. And finally, what if there is a disruption in the fuel that feeds the power plant because of politcal turmoil in the country of origin. Now we are into a very big ring and the complexity gets beyond most peoples understanding. Thank goodness most of our problems in life are not so difficult.

Another use of this rings of system seeing is to understand human behavior. I have used the idea of personal responsibility to demonstrate this. I once asked a group to think of a person in a WWII concentration camp. If they were getting beaten by a guard, would you say that the guard is personally responsible. They all said yes. Then, I asked if the commander of the camp was also responsible. Again yes. Then, how about the other guards that only guarded the fences and never interacted with any prisoners, are they responsible. Probably yes, was the answer. How about the cooks and other civilian service people who maintained the camp for the guards, were they responsible? Now there was some cautious yeses. How about the people in the surrounding community who grew the food, baked the breads, and otherwise gave direct support to the whole camp. The question came up, did the people know what was going on. If yes, they were responsible, if no, maybe. As you can see, this expansion of the rings of system support goes out and out to finally encompass the whole of human activity and you can begin to see that even the most vile actions of humans, is still connected to all of us in some ways. To say it is just one nations problem is to not understand the ring of nation creating. This way of seeing an ever expanding ring of system will quickly bring you to see that we are the world and we are all responsible for what we have created, even if almost all of us have lost sight of that fact.

A PERCEPTUAL INTELLIGENCE STORY

I USED TO HAVE A WONDERFUL DOG named Phoebe, a mixed Lab with a very easy disposition. She also was a great lesson in PI for me. All animals are greatly blessed with PI, for it is this absolute attention to the present environment that gives them the best chance for survival. It lets them know when predators are near by, or where prey may be hiding. Phoebe was a great demonstrator of this for me. Not so much in the hunting or being hunted, since she was always well fed, but in her ability to "see" me.

My favorite story of this is around giving her a bath. I used to live out in the country and I had a large barn like garage that had a water pump next to the door. When I gave Phoebe her bath, it was always at this pump, and of course, she did not like having a bath. So each time I that I wanted to give her one, she would sense it and not come when I called. But, at the same time, this door led into the garage where I parked my truck and Phoebe loved going for rides in the truck. So, one day I figured that rather than going to the pump and calling her for her bath, I would go to the garage and call her to go for a ride. Normally, as soon as I would head to the garage to get in the truck, she would run for the door and stand there rapidly wagging her tail in anticipation of another ride in the truck. But this time, as I headed toward the garage and called for her to go for a ride, she hesitated and by the time I got to the door, I turned around and there she was at the top of the driveway, sitting down, with her ears drooping. She knew it was a ruse to get her down to the pump for a bath. This became a little game between her and I over the years. If I was going for a ride, she was always at the door, and if it was bath time, no matter how I tried to fake it, she would be sitting up there at the top of the drive. It got kind of spooky, since it felt like she was reading my mind. I never fooled her. Not once.

This is PI at work in the animal kingdom. Her little brain was so attentive, she could tell, by some means, what my intentions were. If a dog can be that perceptively intelligent, imagine what we humans could do with our brain, if we got all the conceptual chatter out of the way.

One other aspect that I attribute indirectly to Phoebe was watching her chase rabbits. Here was an example of two competing PI's trying to play out their survival game. As the rabbit would dart back and forth through the woods, Phoebe would be right on her tail, probably tracking the rabbits scent. But here was the interesting PI thing I observed about the rabbit. Once when Phoebe totally lost her track and was circleing in the woods, the rabbit came out into the clearing near where I was sitting. It stopped and began to nibble some new young shoots budding out of the ground. There it sat, calmly eating away, as if nothing in the world was more important. As I watched, it struck me how if we humans had just come out of a race for our very lives, we could not calmly sit down and eat a meal. We would be carrying the "near death" experience with us and replaying in over in our heads. We would be shaking with fear, and worried that something bad may still happen. Not the rabbit, it just sat there eating, now and then perking up its ears and glancing around and then back to those juicy new shoots. Being present with PI, lets us see what is actually happening now, and when the now is a pretador, we run, when that is over, if we see food, we eat. Simple.

I am not saying that we should become animals and live in the forest, but we have lost this wonderful brilliance of our intelligence of being present and sold it off for our ideas. Our ideas and concepts still have a place for us, just not in the forefront of our direct experience of the world. I often wished that I could be as present as Phoebe. I wonder what I would be capable of seeing.

SUMMARY OF PERCEPTUAL INTELLIGENCE

I WOULD WISH THAT BY NOW, you are getting some sense of what I am trying to describe. The actual seeing of processes and systems without any interpretive thought, shows you how the world works. That is all. It is a deeper understanding without judgment And, it also begins to give one insight into why and how many of our bigger human problems persist when no one seems to wish that. The greatest difficulty in using this intelligence is that our conceptual intelligence will desparately want to turn this into another "good" idea. Our CI will want to make this a new right answer to something, even if the question is not very clear. It is the role of CI to know, not to see and understand. It is the role of CI to take a dynamic and un-namable process or system and to name it and nail it down, learn about it, and place it in the memory bank. Then we can sit around and talk about Perceptual Intelligence and turn it into just another filter that blocks our direct experience of the world in front of us.

I am pointing to something that is only in front of you right now and CAN ONLY be in front of you right now. There is no PI in the past and no PI in the future. PI can not tell you what to do or how to be, it is a way of being in itself. Simple awareness is enough. Then with that awareness always at hand, you can use all the CI tools you have at your disposal. Reverse this and put CI first and you simply lose actual life.

The following are some implications and applications of this in our everyday living. Although I have to use the tool of CI to describe this, always remember that I am pointing to what can actually be seen by observation. There is no advocacy in all this, but your CI mental process will want to turn it into that. Do not ever take my words as truth, the truth is before you. Always, in the constant present.

APPLICATION AND IMPLICATIONS OF PI.

PROCESS IMAGES AND SYSTEM IMAGES

MOST RELATIONSHIPS IN THIS WORLD tend to be a relationship of "my image of me in relation to my image of you". This purely conceptual relationship is in actuality no relationship at all between two people. It is mostly happening in the mind of each party and only small bits and pieces of the other are ever directly experienced. The point being that, to have a direct relationship with another is to engage them without personal images of self or other. Without these images then we show up fresh and new as we actually are. Let me take this a little further to add to the complexity that may be necessary to understand as you may attempt to clear yourself of images.

Through some recent conversations, it has become clear that left-brain dominant people (mostly men, but women also) function by creating "process images". A process image is a conceptually designed structure of a role that I identify with. This role is understood in terms of how it plays out linearly. Let me give an example to explain. If I have a process image of myself as boss, then how I understand that image is in the way it carries itself out in a workplace environment. I would have ideas of how I am supposed to act and respond and manage people. This image exists WITHOUT context and stands alone as a "right" process of being a boss. I would also have a process image of employee that matches and compliments my boss image. That would be a mental description of what a good employee does and acts and other critical criteria that I hang onto this process image. Of course, all this is almost completely unconscious to us. So, in engaging of myself with an employee, I am attempting to play out my process image and try to fit the employee into my process image of them. ==If the bits and pieces of actual behavior fit my image then things are fine, and if not then I have a reaction.== There is no right/wrong or good/bad associated with this, only a description of how we work.

What I have come to see is that right brain oriented people (mostly women, but some men) tend to create system images of self and other. By that, I mean that the conceptual notions I have of my various roles include others as embedded aspects of that. It is a highly contextual image of me in the idealized relationship. This is totally different than the process image, which is me as a stand-alone acting entity. The system image then engages with system images of the other, meaning that I understand another as an integrated entity in context of what I think their life is about. We must remember that all this takes place in our own head. As these system images engage, there is a much more complex dance as I gather bits and pieces of actual data. This approach creates much more sympathy and flexibility around what plays out. This is probably why right-brained people in boss roles are often seen as being "too soft" on their people. They understand too much!

Now, what happens when a "process image" person engages in a relationship with a "system image" person? For ease of understanding, lets just call this a man and wife. The man (process image) has clear and non-contextual ideas of what a man and wife should be about. He sees himself as separate from his wife, but connected through this marriage agreement. While the wife, (system image) sees herself as part of her husband and also in relationship with him through this agreement called marriage. As they attempt to communicate about issues, he sees it clearly as a matter of living up to the prescribed roles. I do this and you do that. Meanwhile, the wife sees a contextual me in relation to a contextual him. The roles are not nearly so clear and solutions are not very crisp and clear. ==This is why wives want to talk about the "relationship" while men simply ask, "what do you want?"== For a woman to answer that, she must sort through the me/him and him/me aspect of the relationship. Not always a clear answer, much to frustration of the man and ultimately the frustration of the woman.

Now, no one is a pure process image person nor is anyone a pure system image person. We are a mix, but usually with a tendency toward one or the other. In working on ourselves to drop the images completely, (Back to my initial premise that there is no real relationship when it is image based) it becomes much more difficult for the right brained person to do this. The initial self-observation will reveal that myself consists of contextual others and I cannot separate or find the boundary between other and me. The image contains both. The struggle that ensues is one of feeling that to drop my image is to abandon the other. Of course, this is not actual, since it is all in our head, but it is a very powerful image in our head. For a process image person, it is a simple matter of seeing the image and dropping it with the clarity that I get closer to the other through this process. There is not the sensation of dropping the other also and thereby losing them.

Ultimately, to be present in the world is to show up without images of self or other. I have found that the system image people seem to see the value of this presence more than the process image people. But the road to presence is made more difficult for the system image person and price seems higher to pay. A balanced process/system person seems to have the easiest time of it. For them, they can have enough value to give them energy to pursue this and learn from dropping the process images first, as they build the capability to drop the more intertwined and difficult system images.

SIMPLE PI FACTS

THE FOLLOWING IS A SUMMARY set of facts from the PI perspective. They are not intended to be taken as eternal truth, but as bases for exploration and experimentation. Don't believe them; test them and observe them in your own life and see what emerges.

1. WE ARE THE WORLD. The world of human beings is all of us collectively. There is no "Me" here, and the "rest of you" over there. What we do individually is part of, and integrated with, the entire world of human beings. Our personal process of living is the cause and effect of all humanity. We are causing the world to be, and the world is affecting us.

    Personal note: I have always been amazed at how business executives do not see themselves as part of the organizational system they run, how parents don't see themselves as parts of the family, how teachers don't see themselves as parts of the learning process. We entertain the illusion that we are separate from the world and others and must struggle against them. When we see that we are the world, the struggling against takes on a different meaning. What, indeed, are we struggling against?

2. WE MAKE IT ALL UP. We humans give meaning to things and others. We make up what various events mean to us. We make up the concept "money" and it holds its value for as long as we agree that it's valuable. We make up "rights," put them into a constitutions and give them the force of law. We make up moral and religious codes and present them as divine. We make up boundaries and declare them sovereign states. We make up products and urge them on consumers, telling them life will be better. We make up our identities and

wear them with pride or shame. I make up this list, and could go on indefinitely. We can make up anything we want. These inventions of the imagination are neither good nor evil; they are simply what we do.

3. WE HAVE CONSTANT CHOICE. At every moment we are incapable of not choosing. I can stop typing and get something to eat or take a nap. Right now, I choose to continue. Whether that choice comes from prior conditioning or from free will is not my point. Whether we are making conscious choice or unconscious choice is not my point either. It is simply that we continually make choices.

   Personal note: I remember the old Jack Benny routine, where the mugger puts a gun to Jack's head and says, "Your money or your life!" There's a long silence while Jack looks blankly at the robber. Then the mugger says, "Well?", and Jack replies, "I'm thinking, I'm thinking!" Most of us would say that Jack really didn't have a choice, but the routine reminds us that factually he did. We want our choices to be clear-cut between good and bad, or right and wrong, but in reality they are, like Jack Benny's, between bad and bad, or good and good.

4. THERE IS NO RIGHT WAY. When we notice that the people of the world choose so many different ways of living, we have to ask ourselves, why so many right ways? The fact is, we make up our individual and collective "right way" because experience and hope tells us life will work better that way. We try something new and if it works better than the old way, we adopt it as the new right way. When we do this collectively as a community or a society, we invest it with authority and power, claiming that it is right, not only for ourselves, but for everyone. Simply to say it is a "better" way sounds so tentative and wimpy; we'd rather know that what we're doing is right. I find that "right" is the adopted approach when we can no longer "see" how things work.

   Personal note: The fact is, that if you look at the evolution of science (the "right way" to understand the way the world works), many old "laws" have given way to newer, more accurate understandings. Pursuit of control tends to create the "right way" mentality. At its best, the "right way" is nothing more than the best explanation we have right now for how things work.

5 WE DON'T KNOW THE FUTURE. This fact seems rather obvious. Even the weather forecaster can only give us probabilities. Even so, we have a hard time answering, "I don't know what will happen, where I will be, what others will do, etc." The fact that I don't know doesn't mean I don't prepare for winter or pack for a long trip I intend to take. It does mean, however, that in human relationships, we do not know what will come about. We can best deal with whatever happens by being in the present, in touch with things as they evelove.

<u>Personal note</u>: We waste so much time and energy pondering and worrying about the hypothetical future. As we move through life we need to take occasional directional glances (assuming we know where we want to go), and return back to the present. It is like what we do when we are driving somewhere. We glance at the map now and then, but most of the time we are looking at the road and the conditions present to us.

6 THE WORD IS NOT THE ACTUAL. This is probably one of the most frequently forgotten facts. All it means is that the word "food" is not something you can actually eat. The words we have made up collectively, that constitutes the English language, is for the purpose and ease of communication with all those who speak and write it. These word symbols help us tell each other what we need or want or love or appreciate or see or think. But we all know, when we think about it (which we seldom do) that the symbol is not the thing signified. I never mistake the map I look at for the highway I'm actually driving.

True as this statement may be, we take words for actual people all the time. He is a liberal, she is a bitch, he is a Jew, she is a black, she is a Christian, he is a father, she is a Japanese, he is a redneck,etc. The first step in separating human beings from one another is to turn them into a concept: name them, make up some meaning for the name, and get people to respond to the meaning embodied in the word, rather than to the person named.

We do this to ourselves also. We make up names for ourselves that remove us from the actual human being we are. <u>Life itself cannot be symbolized in a way that is greater than its actual happening</u>. While useful, symbols are less than the actuality they symbolize.

<u>Personal note</u>: I witnessed the effect of naming when I was in the army during the Vietnam era. The first thing done to me was to condition me to the concept of "Gook." I was told I was learning to kill "Gooks," not human beings. All of us have a difficult time killing humans, but once we conceptualize and name, (whatever that name may be) then killing becomes much easier.

THE PARADOX CONNECTION

IF WE DO NOT SEE THIS WORLD paradoxically, either we haven't begun working on our conscious awareness, or we have transcended normal reality.

Those who still believe that there is only one right way to be in this world have not gotten out of themselves to experience another's reality. The first time they do that, cracks appear in the carefully constructed mental walls enclosing a sanctuary from which all others are judged. Staying in this sanctuary invites a lifelong struggle with all other opposing sanctuaries of thought and belief. Many, if not most, seem to believe that life is this struggle. In my view, that is a hellish existence. Unfortunately, society applauds those who struggle, crediting them for "standing up for their beliefs." Most wars are fought over opposing beliefs: both sides stand up for their ideas – until one side knocks the other down. In most cases, the result is only that the losers' beliefs harden.

The first stage of transformation is to crack the wall of the mental sanctuary. Standing in another's shoes is one way to do that. Living in another's reality for even a moment allows one to glimpse the paradoxical nature of life. As we develop compassion, the ability to experience another's suffering, we see more and more of the paradox of multiple realities. Once we are totally confused, we may be able to see the underlying oneness and harmony beyond the paradox. Reality is only experienced as paradoxical when we try to view it from within conceptual intelligence.

Zen masters, seldom understood in our world of linear, rational thought, constantly confront their students with paradox through the use of *koans*. A *koan* is a paradoxical question or statement like, "What is the sound of one hand clapping?" Leaving students in a state of mental unrest, the master prescribes activities like meditation and simple work to center the self. The combination sometimes ushers in a breakthrough beyond the paradox to enlightenment, or expanded Perceptual Intelligence.

The reason why paradox is such an important connecting link is that it forces us to confront the illusion that "we can conceptually know reality". Concepts are simply tools for helping us be here. When the tool dominates, takes the place of reality, we cannot be here in a quality way.

Some of my favorite paradoxes are:
1 I am right that there are no right ways.
2 My greatest desire is to have no desires.
3 The highest value one can hold is to hold no values.
4 Try not to try.
5 When you learn how to do nothing, everything will be available.
6 You can't help being here, and we hardly ever are.
7 Identify with nothing or everything.

Holding two seemingly opposing states in your head at the same time is practice for surrendering to oneness.

MAYBE

IN TIMES OF RAPID AND INCREASING CHANGE, we seem to be prone to large emotional swings. For some people, these swings have become their way of living. They depend on them for their source of enjoyment. (Some really do seem to enjoy a catastrophy!) We also seem to be living in a time when, in organizations and in society as a whole, we must perform at higher levels of skill and productivity than ever before. Achieving such performance, while so many of us are given to wild emotional excess, doubles the required effort, and may not be possible to achieve.

The following story suggests an alternative approach. A Zen master welcomed a traveling stranger into his home. When the stranger left, he gave the master a fin white horse. All the neighbors gathered around and congratulated the master on his good fortune. "Maybe," was all he replied. The next day, his son was riding the horse and it threw him, breaking the young man's leg. "Such misfortune!" cried the neighbors. The master's only response was, "Maybe." The following day, an army came into the village to recruit young men for a battle. They ignored the master's son because of his injury. Once again the neighbors exclaimed at the master's luck, and one again he replied, "Maybe."

The story illustrates that we don't know where events are leading. Whether they are "good" or "bad" remains to be seen. The lesson is to remain present and live in and with the moment (PI) in the face of seeming good fortune or misfortune. Only in a state of "being with" the action of the moment can we see opportunities open up.

When we are caught up in our CI responses to external stimulation we are no longer here. We are up in our heads, judging the rightness or wrongness or goodness or badness of events, just like the villagers in the story. It is difficult to let of this addiction to external stimulation that makes us feel alive and in charge of events. Actually, most of us will not see any good reason or purpose even to try to let go of it. We really enjoy the addiction. We even think it is human nature. It certainly is normal.

In organizations I have witnessed countless hours spent discussing horrible calamities that may occur, as if they were already an accomplished fact. This is another "as if" behavior that ignores the work that needs doing and the learning required to do it. I have also listened to friends worrying about how a new romantic relationship will turn out. "I wonder if he/she will like me?" "I just know they will be angry." –All wasted energy.

Some of us may see PI as an extremely flat and unexciting way to live. I only suggest that you practice and experience being present and disconnected from the stimulation of "as if" for a while. Let your judgment be based on current experience rather than fantasized projection. This way of living must eventually bring us face to face with our fear of nothingness, aloneness, and death. It is this fear, I believe, that we seek to avoid with high stimulation. Embracing, then going through the fear, builds our courage and gives us access to peace and growth.

ROOT CAUSES

WHEN WE LOOK AT LIFE, we usually see the surface, seldom the depths. We are satisfied with seeing simple cause-and-effect relationships. This concept-based framework deals adequately with simple situations. For example, you bake the bread too long and it burns. Nice and simple cause and effect. However, this logic is inadequate when it comes to dealing with the complexity of organizations, relationships and personal life.

In manufacturing, the new intelligence regarding quality requires everyone to dig deeply into the manufacturing process and system to find the "root cause" of breakdowns. Historically we have been satisfied with simple cause-and-effect logic. Is there a problem? Look for the most immediate cause, use a band aid to patch, and get things running again. This thinking has led to endless "fixes" that eventually become part of another cause-and-effect problem and cure. Perceptual Intelligence tells us that "root causes" are often invisible and remote from where the problem surfaces. At the heart of all quality problems in the production of things is the way we think about what we do. That is why the quality "gurus" keep telling American managers to "change the way you think."

Observing from a PI view expands our breadth and depth of seeing. Seemingly endless commentaries on television and in newspapers heap harsh judgment on the way our world is working. Their blame is based on simplistic cause-and-effect analysis. Very little understanding is created, since the commentators seem to be more interested in proclaiming the rightness or wrongness of the situation than in developing an appreciation of how things really work. Why don't we go deeper? Is it simply a matter of "sound bites" or the impatience of viewers with thoughtful, thorough exploration?

I believe this surface approach is partially due to the seductiveness of simplistic logic. An example would be, "things are as they seem to be." Think about how easy it was centuries ago to believe that the sun moves around the earth. You wake up every morning. The sun is in the east, and through the day you watch it as it moves through the zenith to the western horizon. That is proof enough, so the inquiry ends. Then along came Copernicus and Galileo who announced that the earth moves around the sun. General outrage on the part of the learned and distinguished men of their day greeted this announcement.

Why was a challenge to the simple logic system so threatening? In this case, the system must be expanded first to see that the challenge to the logic was really a challenge to the notion that "we human beings are the center of the universe". This was a central assumption of the Christian church at that time, therefore this assertion was seen as rebels attacking the power base of those who controlled the ecclesiastical system. The root cause of the "problem," then, had nothing to do with an attack on the notion that "things are what they seem." Rather, it was related to the need of churchly authority to stay in control.

In manufacturing the case is similar. Most studies have found that the main cause of quality problems is the way managers think about themselves, specifically about their need to maintain [the illusion of] control. Dr. W. Edwards Deming, the late American quality guru, claimed that 80% of all problems are managerial. If that is accurate, it is obvious that one reason we don't like to dig too deeply into the system is that it leads back to those in charge, namely us. Challenging the power always puts one at risk. Galileo was threatened with torture until he publicly renounced his point of view.

On the personal level, why is it so difficult to dive deeply, since there is no one in charge except ourselves? My sense is that we don't like to explore our inner system because we have authority figures within ourselves as ego states. These ego states are ever-willing to judge harshly and threaten when another part of us begins the process of digging into our system to discover the root causes of our behavior. One of the first reactions I get from participants at workshops when starting this digging process is that it is so depressing. What they are experiencing is judgment from the other ego states who feel threatened by observation. We break through this judgmentalism by simply observing the judging ego state from our PI view. Observation without judgment diffuses criticism.

PERSONAL POWER

UNFORTUNATELY, PERSONAL POWER has come to mean power over others, or control over money or things. This is not the kind of power I am referring to. Rather, I mean the power to sustain our Perceptual Intelligence: the power to stay present with the situation at hand and not be distracted by our past conditioning. This mental power is present in all of us at birth. In the process of learning language and differentiating between this and that, our PI degenerates. Without the power of sustained PI we can only have relationships with the past, yet the only actual opportunity for any quality relationship lies in being present.

Following are some practices engaged in by people that diminish their power to stay present. There are no practices that will increase your power; you already have that. What appears to be an increase is merely the removal of a blockage. Once a blockage is removed, we are free to experience the power we have always had. I invite you to drop some of the following blockages.

1. <u>Needing to be sure of the uncertain</u>. This blockage arises when we over-analyze ourselves in an effort to make the "perfect" plan of action. It detracts from our sense of being dynamic in the process at hand and instills needs to hang on to plans already made that may no longer fit. Energy becomes internalized in fighting against acknowledgement that the plan requires

changing. We work hard to avoid the sense of being out of control even when we know we can't control the future.
2. <u>Fear of losing the known</u>. There is no fear of the unknown, but rather the vacuum of the unknown is quickly filled with our fantasies of possible evils and what they would do to us. Usually our fears take the form of losing face, losing security, losing acceptance, losing money, or suffering physical harm. We are attached to our present conditions even when they are not optimal. Energy is consumed in dealing with these fantasies as if they were actually happening. We do not need to give up the knowns we have; rather, we need to understand our relationship to them.
3. <u>Comparing, evaluating, and imitating</u>. These activities combine to sap energy and power from acting in the present with what is actually going on. Evaluating and comparing ourselves against others blocks our power to be what and who we are. In imitating others we give up on our own unique potential and become second-rate copies. This is backed by our belief that we can only be powerful, relative to the power of others. That is a trap.
4. <u>Believing in authorities</u>. This block develops the idea that our personal view of the world is lacking and insufficient. When we hold this view, we lack the energy to act on what we are seeing, because we believe that our perceptions are inadequate. We then spend energy seeking the "right" authority who approves our thoughts or actions, or tells us what to do. There are no authorities about our personal living.
5. <u>Concentrating on ideals, values or identities</u>. Thinking about these mental constructs interferes with our ability to see and act on what is going on before us. Our energy is spent gathering support for our own set of values and ideals, or defending against opposing views. All from the past.
6. <u>Becoming someone or something else</u>. This barrier is based on the notion that what or who we are right now is not good enough, or is not what we want to be. It takes energy to drive ourselves from what we are to what we "should" be, and denies that we have chosen to be where we are right now.

7. <u>Being right</u>. Worry over doing the wrong thing takes great energy that could be used to deal with what we are doing. Trying to be right ensures conflict with the possibility of being wrong.
8. <u>Not letting others have their perceptions</u>. Energy is wasted in trying to force others to see things as we do, then in resisting another's point of view and doubting the validity of our own. This internal ego concern builds a wall against deep communication.
9. <u>Denying responsibility for the life we lead</u>. This barrier is the ultimate energy stealer since we declare to ourselves that we are not in charge of our own living, and are therefore helpless victims. We then constantly react to events external to ourselves, rather than focusing on our experience of those events. We sincerely believe that others make us who we are and how we feel.

There are probably many more energy stealers than those I have listed. To be rid of them is a matter of seeing how they affect our living. This awareness will help us to let them fall away. Trying to move ourselves away from doing all these things involves yet another expenditure of energy. Being fully in the present, without past or future, free from conditioning, is the most powerful position possible. This is PI at its best.

This kind of power is not the kind that goes to war, or influences others to follow a certain way, or believes a certain doctrine, or does the things they "should" do. Power over others, after all, is actually the result of others' denial of their own power. Rather, true power allows the individual to have perspective on his/her own relationship with the world of others, of things, of ideas, and then to make free choices based on that perspective. The powerful person is simply alive in the moment, making choices.

PERSONAL GROWTH AND PI

I THINK IT FITTING that to end this section, I need to explain something about the whole notion of self growth. Many of you may be reading this book for the intention of your own "personal growth". Who is the person who is supposedly growing? I know I have used the word growth several times in this book, but I do not mean it in the normal way it seems to be understood. From a PI perspective, one of the things you notice when you simply look at yourself in the present, is that there is "no self" there. You can observe your being doing many things through out your day, but what you will observe is a human in action. There is nothing more than this flesh and blood in constant movement. You can observe the comings and goings of your thoughts and emotions and see how fleeting they are. What you will not see, is all the images, values, identities, etc that you "claim" as your self. They only exist in your CI mind. They are not actual in the world.

So, if you can see the truth of that, then there can be no self to grow. There is nothing to become, to aspire to, to set a goal for, or even to have some grand intention about. You show up aware and you begin to "see" how all this other stuff is a creation of the CI world to control us, to make us unhappy with where we are, to set up ideals to measure us by, to motivate us toward something, and other means of conditioning us out of simply being present and aware. The kind of growth I am speaking of, is really an allowing the natural growth to take place by unlearning all the stuff that blocks us.

It is similar to a farmer growing a crop. They do not grow corn, even though that is how we speak of it. Corn grows, because it is the nature of corn to grow. Farmers simply prepare the soil, plant, give it some food and water and then get out of the way. Corn grows! It is much the same with us. Our greatest growth is not controlled by some ideas of who we think we should be, where we should go and what we should do.

If we can let our being grow to its natural state, I would bet that it is beyond any concept we may have. We will then be a mature human being. Then from that state of being we can "do" as we wish without ever thinking that our doing will somehow enhance our being. We all have a shot at this mature human being, if only we can get our thinking head out of the way. ==Observe you in all this, and see for yourself.==

PI AND THE DANCE OF RELATIONSHIPS

A NEW PERCEPTION OF RELATIONSHIPS

WHY DO WE HUMANS COME TOGETHER to "relate" to one another in the first place? Until my early thirties, I assumed that, since no one ever discussed it, we all got together to satisfy our needs for security, belonging, safety, and the more unclear needs to impress, seduce, entertain, and compete with one another. We simply used each other to get what we needed. If the exchange of needs was fair and somewhat balanced, a relationship was considered "good."

At the time, I observed that men and women played this "game" of relating somewhat differently. Men more obviously competed and seduced, while covertly they sought security and belonging. Women were typically more open about seeking security and belonging, while in their own way they competed and seduced. That was the game I grew up with and learned to play fairly well. At the same time, I "hid out" within myself as a person behind a mask, who was afraid of not doing well, not being like or loved. Somehow, I thought, once I really learned how to relate, then I could come out from behind my disguise. But the learning always eluded my grasp. So I played the entertainer, and tried to impress by winning arguments. In short, I was normal. I was relating just as all the males around me were relating. Yet I didn't feel that this whole endeavor made much sense.

The women in my world seemed to be caught up in their version of the same thing. They were always seeking someone to "fall in love with" who would make a commitment, so they could ensure their future security. While I was relating to others to get my needs met for winning and owning things, the women I knew were relating to others to get their needs met for belonging to someone, and to own someone as a partner. I don't intend these observations to be judgmental; they are what I observed, and still observe in most of the relating I see going on today. Of course there are exceptions, but essentially I see what I have just recounted to be the foundation of virtually all male/female relating.

This way of relating is based on a CI framework that identifies everything and everyone as some object to be gained, possessed, maintained, and protected for the future, much as we typically treat money and material goods. In my twenties I wanted to be satisfied that I was "right" in my opinions through out-arguing my friends, thus thinking I was gaining their respect and admiration. I protected my self-image concept by being very defensive when any of my positions were questioned. I don't think I was much different from anyone else in this respect.

At age thirty, I got my first PI view of relating when I went to my first training in group dynamics, although the program was not portrayed as such. The training gave me an opportunity to crack the shell of my CI-based view. For the first time I was with a group of people who, though they didn't start there, ended up relating to each other on the basis of nurturance, growth, learning and safety in a way that enabled self-exploration. I now see that this "experimental" way of relating produced a drastic shift in consciousness, one that at the time I scarcely imagined. For the first time, I began to notice the here and now process of people interacting. And for the first time, I confronted the CI images I held inside me.

At the same time, saw that it was possible to slip back from a PI, to a CI-based approach of relating. The group who had had such a wondrous experience of love, power, peace and caring during the training, now wanted to hold on to and possess one another. Instead of learning about what happened, and takng that learning forward into their lives, they wanted to get back together, "keep in touch," maintain the magic that was generated at the workshop. They did not see that this very desire to preserve the process and the resulting heightened relationship would only serve to kill it. ==Conceptualizing is the first step to killing a living relationship.== Group members fell back from the present, where life was, into their conceptual mental world, where things and people were possessed until they suffocated.

I was recently describing this experience to a friend who immediately saw that her support group, originally formed to help women in tough family situations, had regressed to the kind of family they were struggling against initially. My friend's experience indicates to me that though a PI approach to relating is very powerful and fulfilling, it is difficult or impossible to sustain without an accompanying shift in mental framework to overall PI view of living and relating. Our conceptual mind wants to know it and own it.

Through PI awareness, humans come together for the purpose of creating an environment for each other to learn and grow. This idea has some implications for what "being here" is about. It certainly is not about gaining wealth, having a large family, getting famous, becoming powerful over others, guaranteeing personal security or other goals of the material world. Its central idea is that we have unknown potential for growth. In an appropriate nurturing environment, we will, on our own, blossom into something quite rare and wonderful. In the last analysis, we are the farmers of our own soul, and as farmers, we are responsible for creating that environment, an essential element of which is a PI view of relating.

A positive environment for growth requires two elements. First is the need for a place to take root. By that I do not mean "roots" in the material sense of long history, community ties, or a homestead or nation. Instead, ==I mean a positive nurturing "space" where awareness can grow.== In my group dynamics workshop, I found that I was okay simply to be me in the nurturing space the group provided. I did not have to have a great history, be a relative, make future commitments or have a romantic link. Nor did I need to compete for a "rightful place." It was simply a quiet and nurturing place to rest and gain strength. Roots, as I understand the term in this context, are like the kind of bed one requires for a good night's sleep. A good bed is nothing more than a quiet place that gently supports the body so it can rest and be restored.

Second, there needs to be support as one explores and learns about being in the world. In our training we did that by sharing our experiences and by trying out new experiences with each other. The awareness that took place was at our own pace, on our own schedule, based on our own capabilities at the time. It was not a competition, where we constantly compared relative positions on some imaginary growth curve to see who was "best."

From this experience, I learned that we grow as we grow; we do not control that process. A PI view recognizes that some things seem to happen of themselves. We don't need to control everything. As growth occurs, there are times when the current environment is no longer suitable for continued growth. Then we move on as naturally as a duck migrates south for the winter. Migrating south does not make the north bad; it simply does not support needed awareness and life. Ultimately, left to our natural intuition, we will always seek an environment that supports the maturation of our being. Unfortunately, all the values and beliefs conditioned into our conceptual reality, will try to prevent us from making such a choice.

And it is at the point of moving on that most groups and individuals slip back into CI. We feel we have earned the right to keep and possess a group or individual in whom we have "invested" so much of ourselves. We feel betrayed or abandoned by their leaving, as if a departure means we are now discarded and worthless. ==We are so quick to imagine ourselves as nothing more than an object, and then believe others made us feel that way!==

Many of my personal relationships, like those of most others I have known, have resulted in leavings and being left. From family, lovers, friends, professional associates, I have experienced painful partings. I noticed that when I was the one who left, sometimes the other would become angry and spiteful. This negative emotion was explained as the degree of love the person felt for me. Perhaps, but at those times I certainly didn't feel loved. I believe that their emotion stemmed instead from the CI-based view of love that wanted to keep and possess me forever, in some fixed state. I was treated as a thief, who was taking something that belonged to the other person. And I have done the same thing myself to another.

I am saddened that a great deal of psychology justifies and supports this notion of "together forever" as natural and good. It certainly is normal, i.e. the norm, but I am not sure it is natural. The attaching process that occurs in normal relating is similar to training wheels attached to a bike to help children learn to ride. They are fine for a while when we're just learning, but if we're ever truly going to ride a bicycle, those wheels eventually have to be removed. I do not mean to say we must end all supportive relationships; there is just no rule that says we must keep them.

What we don't see when we're dependent upon attachment to another, is that attachment makes both of us into dead material, destroying our ability to simply be and change. Material, according to the second law of thermodynamics, is constantly degenerating, and by mentally attaching ourselves to a CI-based understanding of reality, we too degenerate. When Jesus said, "It is easier for a camel to pass through the eye of a needle, than for a rich man to enter the kingdom of heaven," he was not saying that wealth is evil. He was pointing out that, by ATTACHING ourselves to the possession of money, we essentially cut off our potential for maturing our being. Without maturation, we cannot enter "heaven." But be careful here, it is easy to turn this maturing into another concept like "personal growth" to possess and value. Growth is natural and as soon as we idealize some future "growth" state, we have twarted real maturing.

People ask me how I can live such a lonely and detached life. They assume that, if I am not attached to the CI framework within which they operate, I must be adrift without any "real" connection to the world. My only response is to refer them to my first group experience. Prior to that, I tell them, I never had a true relationship. What I had was an interaction with my own head. I had images of myself interacting with images of others in a constant competition to gain ego satisfaction. I used others, and was used, as material in this game. No here and now relationship was possible, since I was consumed with my words and ideas (and, I suspect, so were most of those I met). To relate from within PI awareness is to be totally with someone as he or she is, without judgment. From that "rooted place," we can help each other learn and explore our beings. In learning and exploring, our "growth" occurs quite of its own accord. In PI awareness, we see we belong to the universe. Loneliness therefore never enters the picture, because we are never alone.

We recognize when it is time to move on, and we take the action without regret, anger, or guilt. I may feel sadness, much like that I experience when watching the sun set on a wonderful day – a sorrow that something beautiful is ending. Yet I know that another different, but equally beautiful, day is beginning. Fully to experience its beauty requires that I be completely present in it as it happens, not preoccupied with nostalgia for the day that is past and gone forever.

THE BIG LIES

VOICES IN OUR POPULAR CULTURE help to keep us stuck in low-quality relationships. Their message is that the normal situation is the only possible situation. This message is simply not true, but it has been so constantly and consistently asserted that we no longer challenge it.

While the message is false, those who repeat it are not consciously lying. They believe it too. They are not evil, deliberately taking us down a false path, for they are victims of the same false belief. Perhaps it is even more damaging to them, since they believe their own falsehoods so sincerely.

What are these falsehoods that bombard us all our lives?

The first is that "others make me feel the way I feel." Popular songs, stories and conversations quietly and persistently condition our minds to look outward to find the sources of our comfort or our pain. We have become disconnected from our inner life, where the power resides to control our emotions. Insetad, we simply react to the external stimulation of others' behavior and become like conditioned machines. To hide this fact from ourselves we have made this machine-like quality of living into a romantic charade. We pretend that this is what "real" relating is about. "when you do this to me I feel good." Obviously, on the purely physical level, we can have simple cause-effect relationships, but when we move to the psychological level, we lose sight of how we actually operate. On this level, we indulge ourselves in romantic ideas of special someone out there who will make all our daydreams come true. In this way we escape from life's actualities. If we don't face the fact that we have responsibility and control over how we use our energy to be in the world, then high quality will not characterize our relationships.

The second lie is that negative expression of energy is natural and healthy. We sincerely believe that we have to get the hate, anger, envy, resentment, and other negative emotions off our chests. We are told that "venting" is good for us. Again, this is a falsehood that originates on the physical level of operating, where, if we do not express pent-up negative energy, but suppress it over a long period, we will experience undesirable effects. What we do not face is that dumping this negative energy has the same detrimental effect on relationships and the larger society. In other words, we poison the world around us by expressing, just as we poison our own bodies by suppressing, this negative energy. The real question then is, how do we not create negative energy when we know that it is like nuclear waste? Once created, it lasts a long time and poisons everything around it. Of course, once we have it we must dispose of it as best we can, but isn't it foolish not to look at the possibility of not creating it in the first place?

Preventing negative energy from being created at all is possible, but not if we continue to believe the falsehood that we must inevitably generate and express it. I know from my own experience that it can be prevented by going to root cause of the negative energy. (Uncovering the root cause is a common tool in managing quality). If we go to root cause, we will find that the source of all negative energy is fear connected to CI.

Here is an illustrative example from my own life. Years ago, I lived with a good friend who had an idea of cleanliness very different from mine. I was neat; he was not. I got angry with him because I was doing all the housework. When I took time to look at this process, I realized that I had a certain concept (rule) about how clean and neat a house should be. My fear was that my roomate was taking advantage of me, because – I thought – he really shared my rules. When I saw that he didn't share my rules, it was absurd to try to make him live by them, I let my resentment and anger go and redirected that negative energy into cleaning the house according to my own specifications. I simply stopped making up this scenario of a malingering roomate who laughed behind my back at this sucker who was doing all his work.

Instead, I did what was necessary to keep my environment clean and neat. (This is the empty boat in everyday life!)

The third lie is that our purpose for living is to get what we need and want. Again, the idea that need satisfaction is the primary driver of human behavior, derives from the physical level of our being. Our bodies certainly have needs for food, shelter, air, sex, water, warmth – those things without which we would not survive. This simple physical fact has formed the basis of how we think about our whole being. We have conditioned ourselves to believe that falsehood. Consequently, we have come to believe that for our psychic survival we need to have recognition, achievement, belonging, status and the like, because we created our CI egos to have those hungers. However, we are much more than our physical bodies.

We are sources of energy that give to, create, and reflect on the world. This energy comes through us, and emanates outward to others. We are in the world to give, not to take. This is obvious when we can simply look at what really happens when we truly live. Test it out in your own experience, as I have tested it out in mine. Given that we are constantly using our energy to be in the world, does that energy make a positive or negative contribution? Is the energy blocked and frustrated or flowing freely through us?

In the longer run, however, I see that those who aim to get do not live in a high quality way. Always needing to get means that we are always feeling empty, like living in a constant state of hunger – hardly a quality state. Even those doing very good deeds in the world are sometimes doing it out of that need to fill an emptiness. That is not the simple giving I am pointing to. What is the quality of the energy coming from you?

WANTING AND NEEDING

AS I HAVE INDICATED ELSEWHERE, relationships in the normal world of material reality are based on need. Our bodies need air and food and water to exist. Without these necessities, we will suffer and eventually die. Everything in the material world needs something. Our car engine needs oil, the flowers and trees need water and sunlight. Simply put, the material world is a world of needs and their satisfaction.

Most of us confuse the ideas of "need" and "want," thinking they are synonymous. They are similar in that that they both express some desire, but the difference becomes clear when we think of the consequences that follow deprivation. If we are deprived of something we need, we will experience severe pain or some other sort of physical suffering. A need denied will not permit us to "get on with living." It will dominate our awareness until we do something about it. Either we satisfy the need or find some way to compensate for, or suppress the pain. In contrast, a want is a concept-based need of the ego. If we are deprived of something we want, we may feel disappointed, but we will get on with living.

Popular notions about "romantic love" tell us that true love requires one person to need another. We sing praises to the pain of a broken heart, and measure the level of "real" caring by the level of distress we feel in the absence of the one we love. These reactions and feelings are certainly real to the people involved. What most of us can't see is that we have lowered our humanness to the physical level of needs. Unfulfilled love leaves us with psychological withdrawal symptoms. Instead of raising our living to the higher level of our conscious mind, we lower our loving to that of just another bodily function.

Most of us sincerely believe that this type of love is the most important part of our living, and the best experience of life itself. It is another example for the CI view. In other words, we idealize the notion of love, compare to where we are in relation to that ideal thought, and react to our relative distance to it. It is how the thinking mind works. In PI reality, there are physical needs and psychological wants. *None* of the wants controls our inner well being. We do not experience jealousy, envy, depression or other withdrawal symptoms associated with need deprivation.

In the PI view, people are whole within themselves, yet part of a greater, universal whole. We want friends, lovers, companions, family or other relationships for the purpose of continuing our own maturing, and helping these others to pursue their being. Not having this want fulfilled does not lead to pain and feelings of rejection, because this reality is one we choose. We are responsible for the living we create. When we do not get a want fulfilled, we simply move on and create the next episode of our living.

In the CI view of reality, the lack of food does make us weak, and cold air does make us shiver, and the lack of water does make us thirsty. It is a cause and effect world, where things outside ourselves do produce internal reactions. The PI-based view accepts the physical level of experience, yet does not let that level dominate the rest of our being. On the psychological level there are no needs. We do not need to become anything, do anything, act any particular way, or feel any particular emotion. Here the key word is "need." We may want to do many different things, but we do not need to do anything. As a matter of fact, doing nothing is the most difficult and most powerful space we can occupy. Then we are simply open and present to the world.

Babies have been shown to need more than pure physical food and comfort to survive and thrive. Why is that not still the case with adults? Infants only have PI; they have yet to create CI. They sense that human connection is important for health, growth and development; their very lives depend on it. Of course, if they do not get this connection they cannot grow and death results. But they are not angry or offended; these emotions belong to the CI view.

All through life, human connection is crucial to our maturing being. Unfortunately, most adults lose the ability to relate successfully to others, since we become so self-centered, imprisoned within our CI view. Infants, on the other hand, are great receivers of human energy through direct contact. Post-infantile humans block the direct transmission of human energy by developing CI. Rediscovering and tapping into PI regains for us this subtle, yet most vital of human needs. And so, we become as a child.....

TAKING FEAR AND ANGER OUT OF RELATIONS

FULLY AWARE HUMANS feel neither anger nor fear. These emotions result from CI taking over our consciousness and creating machine-like reactions. We can witness the truth of this in our own being. The realization came to me one day while I was driving to work. It was a beautiful, clear spring morning and I was in a happy state of mind. Suddenly, someone swerved into my lane and I had to hit the brakes to avoid an accident. I quickly found myself in quite a different mental state. Angrily, I called the other driver unprintable names. Then I became aware of myself. I had gone from happy to angry in a matter of seconds. How had that happened? What I saw in myself was the process common to all anger and fear reactions.

I had a small piece of environmental data (a speeding car cutting into my lane) that triggered a series of internal processes. My PI response was to hit the brakes and avoid a collision. At the same time, I quickly ran the data by my concept of good driving and determined that it violated my conceptual rules, rules I believed everyone should follow. Hence my angry outburst. I also fantasized what might have happened had I not reacted swiftly enough to avoid a collision. My mental image was of human and automobile wreckage strewing the interstate. Hence my fear of a disastrous possibility. Even though that possibility never happens, I responded "as if" it had.

As I dug deeper into my mental change and its cause, I saw that my need to have my driving rules and impose them on others was fear-based. I was afraid of being hurt, being wrong, being taken advantage of. All this fear was constructed by my CI as projections into the future, based on my past. At that moment I saw how self-centered I was. I saw how arrogant I was to insist that others live by my rules. I saw how I gave up my state of well being over to others to control. Laughingly, I let the anger and fear go and returned to my happy state. (This does not mean that we should not have rules of the road, they are there to create order and that is very important to the physical world.)

On later reflection I realized that my reactions were common to virtually everyone. We use others' behavior to justify our angry outbursts. The fact was, I did not know why the other driver was behaving erratically. It may have been a real emergency, like a major road hazard, or he may have simply been careless. What I did know about myself was that I became less careful when I was angry; my attention was on my anger, not to my driving. I may have inadvertently cut someone else off and initiated another series of those reactions I myself had experienced.

Daily, throughout the world we create this reactive fear-anger dance. Each person claiming justification because the other person started it – like kids scuffling on the playground. We don't wake up and move beyond the fear and anger. We call this reactive dance by various names: war, revenge, defending our honor, terrorism. All are justified because "they started it."

Fully aware human beings see that there is no fear in the present. A truly dangerous situation, like stepping on a poisonous snake for example, creates a physical fright response, enabling us to respond quickly, before CI even comes on the scene. This is fortunate, because fear causes paralysis. It is CI's mental picture of what might happen, like my vision of highway wreckage.

Anger expresses our fear that how others live, may do harm to us. We want to control others, be their authorities; yet most of us do not want to be in control of our own lives. We want to impose peace on others, yet internally we know only fear and anger, not peace. With these emotions actively at work, there can be no quality in human relationships.

How do we break this chain of reactive and negative living? How do we respond to a hot coal burning our hand? We simply drop it, let it go. When, for some reason, we find we can't let go of injurious emotions, we must look at why we are so afraid of simply being present as a human, allowing our PI to respond appropriately. If we never see, all our doing will lead to more of the same. (A word of caution at this point. It is very easy for our conceptual thinking mind to take everything I am saying and make it the "right" way. It is how the thinking mind works. If you are harboring any thought that I am saying PI is the right way, then you need to stop and look at how you are creating that conclusion. If you see how that works, you may see what I am pointing to!)

A PI VIEW OF
CAUSE AND EFFECT

THE WORLD OUTSIDE OURSELVES can only have a cause and effect relation to us at the physical level. Psychologically, we can only hurt ourselves. Very young children seem to be affected by psychological abuse, so how can I make this statement? Infants and very young children are extremely vulnerable to taking in and internalizing negative energy from older persons. Theirs is a purely PI awareness, so they are quick to absorb negative messages as they learn how to survive in the world. Some of these messages get buried deeply, and later form part of their CI view as they create their inner world.

There is a Zen saying: the true person is affected by the world as a mosquito affects an iron bull. In the CI view, this statement sounds harsh and unrealistic. We think that the constant reaction to others around us is what relating is all about. You do this and I react with that. You, in turn, react to my action with a reaction of your own, and on it goes until we "work" through the issue, give up and leave, or turn to other occupations. In the CI view we believe that sensitivity is the ability to stay tuned into the actions of others in ways tht let us react to them most appropriately. When we look at the pattern closely, we can see that it is based on a purely mechanical understanding of human interaction. I call it the "billiard ball model" of living. One ball strikes another, setting off a reaction which sets off another, and so on. This certainly happens, and it is unnecessary.

Let's think for a moment what it would be like to live without reacting in this way to others. If we are typical CI-based persons, we would be imagining living in a void, empty of life. For us, life is a series of reactions without which we sincerely believe there is no life at all. We would be totally detached from others, perhaps comatose, certainly reclusive. Without our reactions, we would be joyless, without stimulation. We would encounter difficulty finding a reason to go on living. In the CI-based world, we live for the stimulation of others to keep us feeling something. Without that stimulation we feel lifeless, threatened with nothingness. This view is based on the idea that there is no inner world, emanating from within and sufficient unto itself.

As we develop our PI, we begin to watch the process and system of ourselves, the first thing we see is this constant reaction to the outside world. As we push deeper into that reaction, we see how our CI-based egoic system of beliefs, knowledge, concepts and values creates its ground. For example, someone says something, you like or dislike it based on your past conditioning, and react accordingly. The reactive round begins. As we get behind that reactive system, inside ourselves, we begin to see a quiet center where reactions have no place. We will, possibly for the first time, since we were infants, come to the world from our natural center which is truly in contact with the world, rather than from our CI system. From this clear and calm center we can see that the reactions of our CI-based ego systems are never sensitive to the world around us. Our ego system created by CI stands between the real world and our natural center, provoking our reactions. What appeared before as life and joy will be seen as mechanical pleasure and pain cycles, driven by old conditioning. There is no life in that reactive cycle, just stimulation and response to the past. It is like we began at a young age to build this bubble around us made up of various thought constructs and as we age that gets thicker and thicker, until at some point, we no longer can see through it. We are then blind.

With this in mind, we can see that the "iron bull" is the only way truly to experience the world as it is, instead of through the bias of our historical conditioning. Only then will we experience real love and compassion for the world and others. Only then will we be free from the past that keeps us reactive and mechanical. Only then will we begin to see the true potential of being human.

A PI STANDARD OF RELATING

STANDARDIZATION IS A MAJOR CONCEPT in the management of a quality production process. It means that the most effective process for producing something has been discovered and that everyone employs this process until a demonstrated improvement is found and adopted. The standard constitutes a base upon which to build an ever-improving level of performance.

How might this work in a human relationship? Is it possible for two or more humans to come together and establish a standard for relating that becomes the foundation for growth? I believe there is.

A standard of human relationship could be one that has a minimum of waste. "Waste" in this context would be the constant crises, breakdowns, struggles, and negative energy employed in "fixing" or "repairing" that pervade most of our relationships. This waste has become so prevalent that most of us think working through these issues is what relationships are all about. The literature is full of stories that recount how couples coped with this difficulty or dealt with that crisis, and treat all the negative energy as normal and healthy. We talk about good marriages as those where people have learned to fight well, or have improved communications so they can express their anger with each other. Such improvements may be necessary, but by learning skills to cope with a poor standard of relating, and assuming that standard to be the best there is, we ensure its perpetuation. We like the control we experience by being capable of conflict resolution, and now don't want the conflicts to go away. In fact, we may find conflict to be the chief way we feel alive in a relationship at all!

A higher standard of relating would be one where there is no waste of energy or production of negative energy to poison the environment. This would be a smooth process of relating that holds true peace and harmony as the highest level of being. Such a process requires awareness of our current processes of relating and willingness to explore why we stir up crises, conflict and negative energy. It requires us to watch ourselves in action and simply seek the source of conflict before it is expressed. The root cause is usually found in our CI-based "need" to be right and in control, or in identifying with certain ideas, systems, values external to our being. It is our CI that creates how the world "should" be. The more we let go of these attachments, the more harmony we are able to experience. At first, the letting go may feel like a loss of control and sense of being ungrounded, adrift. That will pass.

It is difficult to get used to the calmness that comes to a life without conflict. We begin to notice that the people with whom we are in relationship will want us to continue the old games of fighting and power struggle. That is to be expected since they still identify themselves with the game, knowing no other way of defining themselves with another. The idea of *just being* with another person, with no struggle or dispute or problem is highly threatening, because for all their lives they have believed that they were representing themselves through these struggles and were honestly expressing their true selves. They believe that *life is a struggle*. If they do not dominate, they will be dominated and lose the fight. So why should any of us give up our old identity with, and attachment to, struggling and winning in order to pursue harmony, especially if we are good at it? What is the payoff? Obviously, it is not to be found in the current system, but in the moving, or possibility of moving, into a healthier system.

To grow, all systems need a surplus of positive energy. Without a surplus, the system will either just maintain itself or, in the case of an energy deficit, go into decline and deterioration. This is true in business operations as well as in personal relationships. If there is no surplus capital to reinvest, there will be no growth. The point in both cases is that we need more positive energy to help us mature beyong our current state of being. Without it, we are either stuck with the status quo, or slip toward dis-solution.

We can increase our portion of positive energy by eliminating the wasted energy that is used up in negative conflict and struggle. From this base of harmony and peace, both within ourselves and with others, we may find our selves moving to higher levels of living. Relating harmoniously is to deal with ourselves and others from a base of awareness of internal and external process. We can watch the patterns of our relating non-judgmentally, and begin to see where we have consistently created negative conditions. The intent here is to discover how we work, not whether that is bad or good. "Bad" and "good" as judgments always come out of our CI-based systems, not out of personal awareness of our own and others' process. With the newly discovered awareness of our relating process and our internal creation process, we can see opportunities for ending our destructive thinking and behavior. At this point, there is nothing to do but stop doing the negative. What emerges is the natural positive energy needed for our own and others' nurturance and growth.

PI AND ENERGY WASTE

WE WASTE A LOT OF ENERGY in our relationships. The energy I refer to is the conscious energy each of us needs to live our lives. Just as our physical body requires energy to move about and perform its functions, our conscious mind requires energy to function properly. For most of my life I squandered this energy on fairly useless pursuits that fed my CI need to know, control, or be right and good. I constantly argued, complained, criticized, or otherwise judged others and the world around me. Using my energy in this way left me with very little to nurture and let my awareness grow. I also had little left over actually to attend to someone else.

Attending to another human requires a high level of presence. We tire quickly from paying attention, because we have already exhausted our energy supply in internal dialogue, and in judging every comment or action we and others make. (I invite you to try simply attending to someone, without starting the internal editorial comment or self-absorbed chatter that feeds your ego. You'll be amazed at how difficult it is).

Why do we waste so much energy on this internal talk? Why can't we just be quiet, let our minds rest and be receptive. To have an uncluttered view of the world around us? I believe it's because we are trying to assert power and control over others as if they were simple physical objects to be manipulated and controlled. Unfortunately, we have considerable experience with the illusion that we can control others, or be controlled by them. For example, if someone says something to us that we perceive as insulting, we react strongly and believe they have caused us the pain we feel. We have come to believe that the linear cause/effect world is operating on us, exercising control over our feelings. She said something awful (cause), and we feel pain (effect). We do not recognize that it is our own internal lack of conscious awareness that allows the reaction to take place. Similarly, we believe we can have the same effect on others. So we waste energy is trying to control others, or in combating other's efforts to control us, whereas, in fact, we have no control over anyone else, and they have none over us, except on the purely physical level. Testing and experiencing this truth will free up an enormous amount of internal energy.

With that freed-up energy we can start to pay attention to others with whom we are in relationship. For the first time, we may have a direct experience of someone else, and that direct experience will be unencumbered by the useless inner chatter that we usually carry on for the purposes of control. The energy we invest in paying attention greatly improves the quality of our experience of others and their experience of us. Old distractions fall away. We may truly hear someone from their point of view, and we may understand their total message. Exchanges of this kind are calm and, at the same time, rather intense. We realize that we never have to rehearse what to say, or debate what is being said by someone else, or defend ourselves from verbal attack. We can just be there, and that is more than enough. It is the most we can be, because all of us is there.

MANAGING RELATIONSHIPS

PEOPLE IN RELATIONSHIPS WITH OTHERS over time become complementarity in their interactions. The name of this complementarity is collusion. Although collusion usually implies some conscious choice about actions, I find that most relationships are unconsciously collusive. Collusion is not limited to humans. Natural systems all evolve to form complementary reinforcements that maintain a balance. This is what we know as "the balance of nature or symbiotic relationships". We are only now beginning, in ecological research, to understand how the balance is constantly managed. I want to explore this complementary nature of relationships, both externally/organizationally and internally/psychologically.

Organizationally, there are similarities to nature. Various departments, functions and individuals over time learn to complement each other by adapting. Each part of the system "fits" the rest of the system. This fit has nothing to do with effectiveness.

The thing to remember is that all elements are interconnected. Although we may look at pieces, we are touching the whole. This happens in all aspects of work life. The culture fits the style, the style fits the structure, the structure fits the processes, the processes fit the systems, the systems fit the work design, the work design fits the plant layout, the layout fits the quality approach, the quality approach fits the delivery process, the delivery process fits the business demands, the business demands fit current economics, the economics fit the societal culture, the societal culture fits the business culture. This may seem obvious, but it is the first thing we forget when starting to change something. Also, since the world is always changing beyond our own endeavors, the overall system is always in tension with itself. To not recognize this tension is to miss a major component.

In our personal relationships, our deep-felt need to be accepted and liked by others drives us to adapt to what seem to be the criteria for acceptance. We experience this early in life as our parents set overt and covert standards of acceptability that mold our behavior to a shape that complements their needs, ideas and general state of being. When the desired "fit" does not occur quickly enough, the child is given strong messages to adapt, i.e. become complementary. The complementary/collusion aspect of the relationship cannot be seen only from the parents' or the child's behavior. Complementarity demands that two or more parties interact. As the child and/or parents grows and changes, we see the struggle involved in breaking down the old collusions. This is the constant tension in an evolving family.

This struggle also occurs within ourselves. As we grow, parts of us change and grind against other parts. This is true physiologically (growing pains) and psychologically as the complementarity of old arrangements is disrupted. Strong components of ourselves have learned over time to be mutually reinforcing. When we are not changing and growing a nice meshing takes place, and we feel fairly aligned and at peace internally. As long as the world can be ignored or stopped from changing we are okay. Unfortunately, the world will not stop changing, and ignoring it is basic insanity.

Some think we are left with a life of struggle and pain if we are to continue to grow and develop. This is true IF your goal is an END STATE OF FIXED ALIGNMENT! It is at this point that our CI need to be right and to know comes into play. On the one hand we have the need to be accepted and liked forcing us to adapt, and on the other the need to be right and to know forcing us to be fixed and stable. We are faced with a basic dilemma.

Our need to be right tells us that there is a certain way to be. Our need to be liked and accepted tells us to be many ways to suit the situation/person/changing expectation. This dilemma underlies all the complementary elements of our experience: our personal life; our families, and our organizations. It creates an important tension that, in the long term, serves our growth.

In business, for example, the tension is between being right about the way we operate internally, and the need for our customers to accept and like our products and services. Either we go crazy trying to meet every customer demand or need, or the customer thinks we are unresponsive if we only give him what we think he/she ought to have.

In personal relationships we struggle to define who we are, then find that others expect very different things from us. Whom to be true to? Inside ourselves we get clear about what one part of us wants and then struggle as the satisfaction of that part goes against other parts of our being. Of all the things that are complementary, these two basic needs seem to be at odds. That is, the need to know who we are and the need to be aligned and consistent. The question is, how to make them complementary? Is it possible to reconcile this struggle?

The change from apparent conflict to complementarity is simple to explain but difficult to carry out in practice. First, the need to be right must be allowed to change to a need to be aware and in process of becoming. The "right" thing is undefinably dynamic. We use the power of needing to be right in a way that attaches itself to an evolving process rather than to a stable certainty. This means a shift from a content (CI) approach to a process/system (PI) approach. It is an acknowledgement that we can not "know" life.

Second, the need to be liked and accepted must be allowed to switch from the need to have others like you, to your need to like and accept them. Also, applying this principle to yourself allows you to deal with the emerging and changing way of your own being. Not needing to be right allows you to express the need to actively like and accept yourself as you are. Your growth and change will happpen of itself, rather than in a controlled way. The judging based on being wrong goes away. You in relationship with you is constantly shifting through changes that no longer indicate unworthiness and wrongness, but rather a clear and adaptable flow of unfolding. Rigidity of parts based on rightness goes away and is replaced by fluidity. Dislike of unworthy parts is replaced with curiosity. You become amazed at the change! You manage it by being with it, not by controlling it. You shape and form as you go. Demands on others to be different are replaced by curiosity about who they are. Judging is replaced by loving attention.

If, at the beginning of this essay, you were expecting to manage relationships through control, you are doubtless disappointed. If you now see that to manage relationships is to let them grow and improve, you've got it! What you eliminate is the collusion not to grow; the collusion to pretend to be in control; the collusion to believe that there are right ways to be in the world; the collusion to deny the inevitability of change. With the negation of all this conceptual content, you begin to "see" more clearly the dance you are in. This is Perceptual Intelligence at work.

MECHANICAL RELATIONSHIPS

A CI VIEW OF THE WORLD is clung to because we desperately want predictability in life. That is, we want life to obey certain simple laws of cause and effect that we can learn and follow to be happy and secure. We also hate to be treated that way; the idea of our being predictable like machines deeply offends our sense of being human. Nevertheless, our everyday living demonstrates our overwhelming desire to deal with the world and others as mechanical objects. Why is that so?

Mechanisms follow neat cause-effect, predictable patterns. In a mechanistic world we can "prove" who or what is right, who did what wrong to whom. We can choose sides and debate the way the world should be. We can claim "rights" that should be respected and responded to by others in certain appropriate ways. We can tell others how they should live, and what they should believe. We believe that every question has a right answer, and that the mark of an educated or competent person is that he or she has that right answer. So we strongly dislike it when someone makes a choice or responds to a question that reflects a very different perspective on reality from our own.

I once saw a fat woman on television who liked being obese. The audience clearly wanted her to be thin. Various members were concerned about her health, her happiness, her agility and flexibility, and on and on. Quite apparently they did not approve her different choice of personal appearance. Reflecting on this incident, I thought the audience was probably concerned about their own choices. Had they spent countless hours on diets and exercise because they had bought into the lie that "thin makes us happy"? Here was a woman who evidently was happy, and she was fat! No one likes to be duped. Perhaps they felt they had to make her wrong, since, to let her be right in her choice brought their own choices into question.

I believe that many of us are afraid that we have made some seriously mistaken choices in our lives. Rather than face the prospect of choosing again, with all that implies, we vigorously defend the rightness of our original choices. To admit doubt is to suggest a wasted life, which might lead to depression or some other terrible consequence. So we struggle on, desperately trying to make everything and everyone mechanical and controllable. CI is driven by the need to know and control.

By definition, mechanical relationships tolerate a limited arena of quality. That is, mechanical relationships can be quite enjoyable for short periods of time when the people involved are nicely matched. They agree and disagree about the same things, like and dislike the same people, are sexually compatible, play complementary roles. They function well in all their parts like a newly manufactured automobile. The problem is, cars don't alter their condition except through use, whereas humans are constantly altering their states of being. Before long, mechanical relationships between human beings develop friction, and energy is wasted in trying to restore the frictionless state. But one of the laws of mechanics is that things tend toward breakdown, or entropy, and the same is true of mechanical relationships. To reverse this tendency, we are advised by counselors, themselves participants in the mechanical, CI-based view, to invest even more energy in making the relationship "work," because commitment to the relationship is what is important; it is the only healthy way to live. They sincerely believe that.

I have seen the same thing in factories. Good people work in energy wasting unhealthy, yet profitable systems. Since profitability is the only valued measure, nothing else counts. When people question the systems or intuitively know that something is wrong, they are looked upon as disloyal troublemakers. When simply going to work everyday becomes a burdensome chore, because of the stress and frustration, they are judged to be unmotivated. When other interests outside the factory take their energy in new directions, they are seen as not committed. Meanwhile, the mechanical system they suffer under is never questioned.

A PI-based relationship changes the entire situation. People truly in relationship with one another are more curious than judgmental. Women who are happy in their obesity are asked how they deal with the world, and what we can do to help them deal with it more easily. Differences define the parameters of the system supporting humans being human. We do not have to defend or sell our differences in hopes that others will adopt them. Getting others to conform to our practices is irrelevant, since no one has the illusion that one is in some way better than someone else.

Here someone may say, "All that is fine so long as the difference doesn't hurt someone else." This statement comes form the cause-effect mechanical world. When we do something that hurts someone physically, we pay the consequences. (Actually, I believe it can be shown that virtually all negative actions are a consequence of the CI-based view of relationships, specifically notions of control and ownership or possession of others). Psychologically, there is no simple cause and effect mechanical relationship between people. Others do not hurt us and make us what we are. Conversely, neither do they make us something more than what we are. As adults, we are not Pygmalions, the creatures of someone else. You and I are whole in ourselves. In relationship, we come together to help each other become more conscious of our wholeness and the larger Whole to which we belong. We see that fragmentation and separation is an effort to distinguish ourselves from others.

The notion that relationships are based on the cause-effect mechanical model will die very slowly. Song lyrics, commercials, news media, the everyday messages of popular culture assume and promote the CI view. I have no interest in counter-selling PI. I just invite us all to look inward to observe how we operate. Watching is the first step. Not judging what we see is the second. Once those two steps are taken, the rest follows, so long as we resist the temptation to fix whatever we see.

Our desire to fix is always based on the underlying judgment that our or your current state is wrong based on some comparison to an ideal state. No matter how much we insist that "fixing" is simply improving ourselves, the fact is that our underlying urge is to control ourselves and others mechanically. Though our intentions may be improvement, the framework within which we approach our efforts robs us of our humanity.

When we relate to ourselves non-mechanically and non-judgmentally for a few days, we will notice a significant difference. With much practice of this kind of watching and relating, we can begin to relate to the rest of the world in the same way.

WHY WE LIKE MECHANICAL RELATIONSHIPS

I LIKE TO USE THE ANALOGY OF SAILING to explain a PI relationship to the world. Excellent sailors learn to be "with" the environment and the boat. Their work is constantly to integrate their own purpose (reaching some destination) with the wind, ocean currents and the operating characteristics of the boat. This combination of forces permits movement in the desired direction. Sailors do not set themselves and their boats against the sea as an enemy to be conquered, nor to they think that, because they can steer a course across the water, they are in control of the environment. Death and destruction lurk in such notions. Humility and respect are appropriate responses to the immense power of these elemental forces.

Instead of learning from the ancient art of sailing, we have turned away from its approach to the mechanical world of power and control. We liken ourselves to "motor boats," indifferent to the environment surrounding us. For most of us it is a matter of taking a straight course to the destination and going for it with full throttle. We believe this different, direct, approach represents progress over the older, less direct approach that works <u>with</u>, rather than in defiance of nature. In the CI-based view of physical things, it is an improvement. But when we apply the same principles to our psychological living, to say nothing of the natural environment of which we are parts and not the masters, we inflict great harm.

The motor boat analogy illustrates the illusion that we can, through brute force, achieve the peace and security that has eluded humankind for centuries. We delude ourselves that the world is a simple mechanical cause-effect place that can be conditioned to respond to more pressure on the throttle, that we can get what we want through more conditioning and application of mechanical power. At the same time, we like to believe that we are above this mechanistic way of living, even as we want to know how tomorrow will turn out, want to be sure of the security of our possessions, want to be right about our opinions of how things and people should be. We want to impose mechanical control on the world so we won't have to deal with the now moment that is alive, complex and unpredictable.

Similarly, with respect to others, we like our relationships to be mechanical so we can control them to get what we want without being awake to what is actually happening. Getting what we want may sound like a good achievement to most people, but what we do to others reflects what we do to ourselves. To treat ourselves and others as mechanical is to erect strong barriers to awareness of our true selves.

If that is the case, why do we like to live this way? What has happened to us to attract us to mechanical existence, even when we can see the harm it does? I believe we like to live in illusion because the fear of living without illusion is overpowering. Going back to the analogy of sailing on the open sea, sailors do not fear the sea, but they do have tremendous respect for it. Fear would keep them venturing forth in the first place. At the other extreme, foolish bravado would probably lead to shipwreck and disaster. Most of us either fear living, or cover over our fear with heedless indifference.

What is the source of this fear? At what point does it take root in us? Almost certainly it is born and perpetuated through our parents' fear for our safety and felt need to control our behavior. At an early age, we are conditioned through fear. The power parents typically use is the power to withhold approval and diminish our sense of secure belonging in the world. The method is to make us as children, believe that we must "earn" our parents' love.

Having to earn love, rather than having it given freely and unconditionally, plants the seeds of doubt that we really do belong, and drives an unending quest for security. We delude ourselves by thinking that this security will come when we are able to predict and control the future to gain and hold the love we crave. Rather, the only true security is that of being unconditionally loving right now, towards ourselves and others.

With this security we are able to live fully in the present, capable of great growth and full realization of our potential. We don't have to do or be anything other than what we are. There is nothing to earn, sell or barter. We are not in control, but we can be ready for whatever arrives, even a storm at sea.

We do not have to earn love. It is always there to give, so there is nothing to do to get it. Even so, it is hard to do nothing when we feel fearful of nothingness. In such a state of fear we grasp for power to control, and once again remove ourselves from ourselves and the acceptance and love at our heart's core. We have been conditioned well. In every time and place, men and women have written about their need for love and happiness. Scholars tell us that is through the "right" conditions that we will find peace and joy in our lives. Political leaders tell us it is through the strong belief in our "righteous cause" that we will achieve security in the world. Religious leaders tell us that it is in striving against sin that we will "earn" god's forgiveness and favor. Humanitarians lecture us on doing good deeds to "save" the world from evildoers. All are simply more conditions that we must meet to be worthy of the love we need, but never give or get as a free gift.

Conditional love, based on CI, will never create in us an awareness of unconditional love. Conditions are always set for the purpose of control. What we have learned, through the absence of unconditional love, is the love of control. Because of our love of control, we continue to create mechanical relationships with others and with ourselves. It is through control that we experience the illusion of power. It is in this feeling of power that we glimpse the (counterfeit) feeling of love and peace, but it is always presented to us as a promise, not as an actuality. So the drive for power never ends.

What does a boat have to do to float? Nothing! It's the nature of boats to float when they sit, empty, in the water. When we fill our "hulls" with too much striving and desiring, and knowing, and fear, we lose our natural flotation. To float is to walk lightly in the world. When we let go of all the fears based on CI, we experience the essential quality of direct engagement with the world.

CONFLICT IN THE QUALITY OF RELATIONSHIP

IN A CI-BASED RELATIONSHIP, conflict is one of the most important contributors to long term breakdown. The concept of relationship as possession and ownership causes conflict to be greatly feared, because it carries with it the threat of losing what we have. At the same time, our closely held ideas of how things and others are supposed to be and act, makes us feel angry or hurt when those ideas are violated. We are caught between wanting to lash out to defend our violated ideas, and not wanting to jeopardize the relationship with the person who violates them. This inner conflict builds until we finally explode, usually at precisely the person whose affections we least want to alienate. Nevertheless, we feel justified, because he/she made me feel the way we do. At the same time, we're afraid that this is the last straw, and we may have driven him/her away forever. ("You Always Hurt the One You Love")

This combination of fear and anger usually leads to poor communication; we'd rather not speak at all, or tell lies about how we're feeling, rather than risk severing the relationship. But poor communication solves nothing, because the other person, sensing that something is not right, becomes reactive and defensive, thus heightening tension and suspicion, which leads either to conflict or to increased distance and coldness. In such a case, true resolution never takes place. Instead, differences are compromised, or simply allowed to pass from memory – though it is doubtful that they are ever really forgotten. They serve, rather, as bricks in the wall of separation, or as ammunition to use when other differences arise.

Compromise is usually a "giving up" of part of the issue on both sides as a condition for the cessation of hostilities. In such a situation, compromise is not an agreement to support each other in working through the issue, but an agreement to no longer hurt each other – at least not right now.

In PI-based relationships, we see the maturing and support of the people in the relationship as more important than our own personal ideas of how others or things are supposed to be. Moreover, since we do not assume that we own or possess a person in the first place, we do not fear their potential loss. Therefore, there is no reason for conflict ever to arise, because there is no ground in which conflict can take root and grow.

There are times when a PI-based person must deal with a CI-based person. In this situation, the CI-based person will feel all the frustration described above, and will express normal anger and fear toward the other. But in this case, the PI-based person will not react defensively, escalating the conflict. Instead, he/she only desires to help the other learn and grow from the situation. So the response may appear to be passive, allowing the other to vent before moving on, but the PI-based person is actually actively compassionate.

To explain further, when we are PI-based, we know that we are responsible for creating how we feel; therefore we know that we don't have to react defensively. We also know that something painful is going on inside the other person, and that he happens to be taking it out on us. So we simply listen to his struggle. We don't run, defend, apologize, counterattack, or take any action whatever to reinforce the other's idea that "something or someone out there made me feel the way I do." Our outward lack of reaction is not a cold dismissal of the person and his struggle, we are fully there, with the person, but are not colluding with his view that he is justified in attacking us when his ideas are violated. We know that ideas are not more real and important than the real person right in front of us at the moment. Just the opposite.

Often, the CI-based person will be confused. Our calmness contradicts his notion of how a fight is supposed to be waged; on the other hand, his fears of losing our regard and acceptance are quieted. This confusion may cause breakthrough into the PI-based perception of reality.

ATTACHMENTS AND COMMITMENT

ONE OF THE BY-PRODUCTS of an individual trying to ensure future security is that he/she becomes attached. Attachment is simply becoming strongly connected to some thing, person or concept as a guarantor of one's well being. Such a strong connection or identification with something or someone else is often mistaken or confused with the idea of commitment. For some people, the attachment itself is more important than the actualities surrounding them.

I find that most people I know become so attached to their concepts of family and husband or wife that they miss the actual changes going on in the family members. They connect and identify with certain prescribed roles in an effort to control how they and others are supposed to act. (Good fathers always do this; good wives always do that; and so on.) This attachment to fixed concepts is the main deterrent to continued change and growth. Such concepts anchor those attached to them, to the past. The cornerstone of Conceptual Intelligence is to find out the "right idea/image" and identify and attach to it. It is the whole point of conceptually trying to figure out the world so we can do it right!

When I have discussed this issue with people, their initial reaction is that, without these strong attachments there would be no commitment. They judge their commitment by the strength of their attachment. My question is, commitment to what? If we want commitment to concepts about how we and others should be, then we are committed to making people into objects; we make the <u>idea</u> of them more important than the flesh and blood alive persons they are.

And because we are attached to the concept rather than seeing the person, we get frustrated when our family members don't live up to our idea of who they should be. (Kids don't get the grades they should; husbands should be home by 6 so they can play with the children; wives should always look pretty and the house should always be clean.) Our frustration is tied to our need to make the world and others live up to our concepts. We don't really want to hear what the actual human beings in our lives are thinking, feeling, experiencing. We only want them to become our concept of them.

If we want commitment to the interaction between people and a joint increase in the quality of living, we don't need attachments to concepts. We need an ability to hear others in a real-time sense. This ability takes commitment to being present with another without looking at him or her through our concepts of how they should be. The commitment to a quality of living is a commitment to growth and continuous improvement. It is not an end state to which we can attach ourselves.

Tom Lane

ALL WARS BEGIN AS CONCEPTS

THERE ARE MANY WONDERFUL THINGS that have been created by our collective conceptual intelligence. All of our modern conviences, technologies, and the material world we live in. The downside of all this, is that we have been equally good at creating war and suffering. It all begins as a concept. Just like the innovator who visualizes the latest technical breakthrough and then uses her knowledge and understanding to bring it into being, our social world is run by people who have conceptual ideals that they use to determine how the world should be and therefore who are our enemies. As long as we have had a written history, it is a story of war.

Before people lived in a CI world, they surely had battles over food, water, or other means of survival. It is the animal nature of us. But, these were not battles or wars over a religious belief, a racial pride, an economic system or other conceptually derived reason. We needed to survive and when we had the means to do that, we stopped and enjoyed it. Of course, we may have been attacked by another group that lacked what we had. But none of that compares to the misery and suffering we created after we found "ideas" to be a reason for war.

On a smaller scale, we have always conducted war by getting the soldiers to objectify the enemy by conceptualizing them. When I went into the Army during Viet Nam conflict, the first thing I was told was that I was going to kill "gooks", "slopes", and other terms to dehumanize the enemy. Why do we do that? Simply because it is hard for us to kill fathers, sons, and brothers. We are fathers, sons and brothers, so we must not have that connection to the enemy. They are evil, subhuman, godless, hateful, deceitful, and any other concept that turns them into an object of possible destruction. All nations, all armies, all religions, and all races have done this to each other. It is what lets us kill.

And we have done this between the sexes. When men are accused of "objectifying women", it simply means that we form a concept about the woman, and we no longer see the woman, we see our idea of the woman. I once watched a show on rehabilitation of rapists in a prison and the therapist asked the men how they depicted the women they attacked. They all used words that were derogatory and demeaning and generalized. Asked what they would do if someone thought this way about their sister or mother, they all said they would be outraged. You see, their mother and sister were real people, their victims were concepts. It is what we do to enable us to commit the most horrible of crimes.

Hitler had most of the German population believing in the concept of Jew as evil. How else could they have done what they did. We have done it with blacks and native americans in this country. Every nation, religion, group. race, and sex has done this. And the worst part is that we even do it to ourself.

The petty wars we have inside our being come from one conceptual image of our identity fighting with another conceptual image. We internally judge and berate ourself for not living up to certain standards. We can even kill our living body, if the wars rage too strongly and too long. We have convinced our self that we are these ideas of ourself. And just like the rest of the world, we do battle with them. We are not a concept. But that means absolutely nothing unless you can see that with great clarity for yourself. To make it another belief will just add more fuel to the fire.

PERCEPTUAL INTELLIGENCE AND COMMUNICATION

DEBATE VERSUS DIALOGUE

MUCH OF OUR COMMUNICATION, beyond simple information sharing, is in the form of debate. Debate is a contest or competition of ideas. We begin with a position, defend it, attack contrary positions, and attempt to solidify our rightness. There is no coming together, only a pushing apart. Listen to all the political debates and you will see how this works. We love our debates as an exercise of our CI skill. We believe that the conceptual ability that is displayed in debate, is proof of the rightness of our ideas. Underlying all debate is the hidden assertion that there is a "right" answer to all of life's issues and problems. Debate is a form of control or simply a "war of words", but still a battle for power.

PI is about dialogue. Dialogue is a process of bringing people together to use the tool of thinking as a way of exploring in unity. A dialogue begins with a question, and both sides join together to explore a deeper understanding of that question. Inquiry is made together to uncover root causes of issues, to really find out how things work. There is no moral judgment or self righteousness going on. It is to understand with clarity and see to the heart of the issue before any solutions are offered. Socrates was put to death in ancient Greece for teaching this dialogue process. It was considered "corruption of the youth" by the powers that be at that time. I wonder if you can see why such a process could be deemed a corruption? What happens when you go beyond the "positions put forth by the powers that be" and look into the process behind that. To explore the system that keeps unhealthy activities alive and thriving. To go into the way we have been taught to think and how that leads us to great contradictions in our living. We say one thing and consistently do the opposite. Why is this corrupting" Do you see it?

Dialogue, when taken to it's natural conclusions will always reveal the dualistic underpining of the thought created world. Every good and moral platitude has in it, its exact opposite. Dialogue will always bring you to a paradox. The paradox that is inherent in the thinking mind. Again, this does not mean that "thinking" is not a useful tool. It obviously helps us in so many ways, but the tool has taken over the human and that leads to great problems. Debate is a form of power over and domination. Dialogue is a road to understanding and wisdom. Which to you choose?

Contrast of debate and dialogue:

DEBATE	DIALOGUE
* Begins with a position	* Begins with a question
* Seeks rightness	* Seeks understanding
* Competitive	* Cooperative
* Defends and attacks	* Explores and uncovers
* Concludes with "winners" or "losers"	* Concludes when both can go no deeper.

ALL TALKING IS TALKING TO OUR SELF

WHEN WE COMMUNICATE TO ANOTHER, of course our intention is to express or convey some information or ideas or understandings to another, but the simple fact is that all talking is talking to our self. To see this we must slow down the process a bit and use our PI capability.

We begin by having an experience or an idea that we want to share. To do that, we must select the appropriate words (symbols of the actual or in some cases symbols of the abstract) that we believe most accurately represent what we want to say. These word choices come from our understanding and our reality and therefore we choose them because they make sense to us. This is the first talking to our self. It is virtually impossible to talk any other way, meaning to talk in some way that makes no sense to us, the speaker. (Except when we are babbling) So, we take these words and speak them (or write them like this) and hope to convey what we understand. This all happens in a split second, so to see this you must slow your process down.

Once the words are put out into space (voiced or written) then the receiver hears them and translates the meaning into the context of their reality and their definitions of the words. There is no other way we can understand anything given to us in this symbolic worded way. This is how our CI works. The content or meanings all come from our CI.

So, we essentially talk to our self with the interpreted input and derive our meaning in our context to make sense of it. We then attribute the meaning to the person who is speaking instead of recognizing that it is us, speaking to our self. This is true, even if your interpretation and definition totally fits the original speaker! Then to respond, we do the same as the initial sender in terms of formulating the message based on what makes sense to me.

"So what", you may ask. First of all, it can slow you down to try to communicate in ways more closely related to whom you are speaking. Secondly, it can show you why people with very different contexts have a very hard time communicating to each other. A context is our personal content system. Thirdly, it shows the value of developing shared context and understandings of words and meanings in order to communicate effectively. On simple sharing of information, this may be a minor problem, but when you go to more complex sharing of life, this can be very difficult.

I have written about PI for quite a long time and the responses I get vary widely, not based on what I wrote, but on their interpretation. I speak to myself in the way I make sense of this experience of life, you hear it and translate it into your understanding and speak to your self as to what I said. All talking is talking to your self. This is not good or bad, only how it works. The really neat thing is, if you watch what you say or how you understand, it will tell a lot about how you work and the context of your life.

EVERYTHING IS PERFECT

I ALWAYS LIKED TO THROW "everything is perfect" statement out to a group of people in my sessions. Their initial reaction is always a roll of the eyes and shrug of "come on, get serious". I would do this to demonstrate how we automatically go to our CI understanding when confronted with just about anything. If you took the term "everything is perfect" from a content side, then it is an absurd statement. For our content or CI mind is always in a comparative and judging mode. So if I say "everything is perfect" then you would immediately imagine many things that do not meet your definition of an ideal state (perfect). It would simply be nonsense. But look at it from a PI view for a bit.

Remember PI only sees the operation of process and system without judgment. The example I would give to a group was "if you put a hamburger on a very hot grill for an hour, what would you get?" Everyone would immediately say, a burnt and charred hockey puck, or something to the equivalent. And of course, they would be correct. Now, I would ask, if you did that 20 times what would you get? And of course you get 20 of the burnt pucks. So, I would say, that is a perfect process for getting burnt meat. If you want to actually eat the hamburger, you have to change the process. Now, that sounds simplistic and maybe even a bit of playing with words. But it is of extreme importance in understanding how things work.

When I would work in factories I would use this the same way. If an operation had a history of 3% scrap, I would say that they have a perfect process for producing 3% scrap. The plant manager would protest, but I would just point out the fact of the matter. Now, he did not want that scrap, but it was fairly constant. Why? Because he and his workers would not look at the process in any detail and persistence without judging, blaming, and turning the understanding into a debate of fault. The solutions were never achieved because the content and judging mind would always derail the exploring. For as soon as we look at something that is "not working right", our whole attitude becomes one of finding the guilty party and that creates defensiveness and covering up of information.

I have observed the same thing when a person looks at their own behavior. If they have a repeated pattern of something they do not like about them self, then I would say that they have a perfect process for doing that. Of course, they protest that they do not like doing that. But, if we keep doing it, then it is perfect. If you can simply observe your process without judging you will get some clarity about how you work. What triggers you, what upsets you, what situations you can not handle. At that point, with that detailed clarity, you then look at the internal thinking processes that are brought into play at those times. This is your internal CI content. It is, what I call the many internal players or actors that inhabit us. We can never move past those until we are capable of totally looking at them without judgment. We have to make ourself perfect before we will see the opportunity to make our self different. Can you see that?

WE ALWAYS ARE DOING WHAT WE WANT TO DO

THIS IS ANOTHER OF THOSE STATEMENTS like "everything is perfect" that stops people short when they first hear it. In our CI mind, there are many things we can think of that we don't want to do, but do anyhow. But if you slow your thinking down and look at the process of our doing, you will see that there can be no other way. I use a simple matrix to show this. Across the top is things I do and things I do not do and down the sides are things I want and do not want. So we get four boxes. 1. Do and want to do. 2. Do and don't want to do. 3. Don't do and want to do. 4. Don't do and don't want to do. Then I ask the participants to put stuff into all four boxes that represent their living.

I begin with the second box of things we do and don't want to do. I get examples like go to meetings, pay taxes, and many other undesirable things of daily life. But, if we slow down and look at the moment of choice when asked to do this undesirable act, what we really do is weigh the pros and cons and we make a choice based on what we want to do. Take paying taxes, I tell people that they do not have to pay taxes, but what may happen if you do not? They respond that they may get in trouble with the IRS or worse. So, at that moment of choosing to pay taxes, we choose between paying and getting in trouble. We do no want the trouble, so we choose to pay. We are doing what we want to do.

In the third box where we don't do, but want to do, it is the same thing. Slow down to the exact moment of choosing and you will see. Take dieting as a common example. We want to eat better, but we continue with the junk food. Well, at the moment of choosing where you will eat, you make the unconscious decision to go off the diet and eat the burger. We rationalize it away, of course. Test this for yourself and look at the moment you make the choice and see if you are not always choosing to do just what you want to do.

In the fourth box, of not wanting and not doing, we sometimes feel guilty about it. Like going to visit a sick co-worker in the hospital. We really don't want to go, and we don't and then feel guilty the next day. There are many things that we don't do and don't want to do that do not matter for us, so that is not what I am speaking to. But at the point of choice, we did something else because we wanted to do that more. Simple as that.

Now why is it important to "see" the truth of this? When we pretend that we are made to do things or are blocked from doing things we want, we waste energy. I call boxes 2,3, and 4 the "whine boxes". When you see that you are always choosing to do what you want to do, then you simply own your decisions and get on with it. No whining, no excuses, no guilt, and no loss of energy. We just choose and do. Life gets much simpler when you use your PI and see how you actually work.

SPIRITUALITY AND PERCEPTUAL INTELLIGENCE

I JUST RECEIVED ANOTHER FLYER on a conference on enlightenment and spirituality. I have been to a few of these and what I find is mostly people trying to leapfrog their psychological work to gain some peace of mind in spirit. I have watched many wounded people desperately trying to find spirit instead of doing their own work. It does not work that way. Spirit is not something to be gained, developed, grown, enhanced, discovered within, brought forth, released, or any other of the babble put forth by most of these presenters. Spirit is already in everything and everywhere and it is only in our awakening that it is experienced.

Awakening to our PI is a tough sell, since the thing that we awaken from is the sleeping sense of self. We have an entire world geared around enhancing and supporting the self and therefore, awakening will never be popular. It simply goes against the grain.

To awaken PI and experience spirit, we need to let go of the self that desires to be awake and seek spirit. We need to let go of the self that wants high esteem. Let go of the self that wants to make a difference. Let go of the self that wants to identify with a religion or country. Let go of the self that wants to achieve fame or fortune. Let go of the self that wants to be approved or wants to approve others. Let go of the self that wants to be loved or to love. Let go of the self that wants to be attractive or attracted to. Let go of the self that wants to believe in God or not believe in God. (God does not care either way) Let go of the self that wants recognition for being good. Let go of the self that wants to be special. Let go of the self that wants to be remembered. Let go of the self that wants to be nurturing. Let go of the self that wants to be helpful and supportive. Let go of the self that cares about the world.

Now stop and observe yourself right now. Is there a reaction to that list of "letting go"? What are you saying inside your head right now? Are you arguing for the virtues that I have made claim to needing to let go of? If you are, then you missed the point completely. The virtues are fine, it is where they reside that is the problem. None of these virtues is a virtue if it resides in a "self". It is just another form of selfishness. By the way, if you were noticing, all the letting go things are positive (mostly). It is the positive stuff that is difficult to let go of. Let go of that and the negative will also disappear since they are two sides of the same coin.

To touch the spirit within is to do the dismantling of our "selfness" and when all that is gone, what you have left is spirit. Spirit is the energy of PI. It was what you came into this world with before you did all the "self construction". Now it is time to "self destruct" our way back to original spirit. I have said this before, "negation is the most positive act" for to negate everything is to have an absolute clarity that without conditioning we are ultimately good and beautiful. This is the realm of spirit and not self. In this realm of spirit you may do all those above mentioned virtues, or none, and you would not be "self conscious" of doing them. It would just be what you see as obvious to do. The virtuous person does not know they are virtuous.

How do we do this? Unfortunately, there is no method since each of us has a unique self-construction that must be dismantled. First, though is to simply "see" the illusion of this named self, not in a judging way, but just in a clear and obvious way. We are not our conditioned self. If this cannot be seen, then all the rest is a waste of time. If you see this illusion, then it is only a matter of observing the various selves that arise in every day living and no longer identifying or attaching to them. This is not easy since the CI self will protest loudly and strongly. It has to since it means their death. Persevere, since it is worth it to live without the self and regain the ever-present PI spirit.

QUALITY AND LOVE

QUALITY AND LOVE come from the PI-based way of looking at the world. I once met a Buddhist at a workshop, and we became friends. One day while walking with my friend, I asked him how he looked at love. He smiled and replied, "If you found a bird tangled in a bush, would you not go and help it free itself? And when it was in your grasp, would you crush it to your chest? Or, if you loved it, would you let it fly freely into the sky where it belonged?"

From a PI-based view, we come together in a loving way, first to help each other "untangle" from the conceptual conditions we were raised with. These are the things that keep us from taking our natural progression and maturing. These are our attachments, identities, narrow rules and negative shoulds that cut us off from our true self. Once we are untangled, real love coaxes and encourages us to exercise our newly freed wings and fly to new heights. We don't clutch and hold on desperately to the other; neither do we push away or cast out. But we take a true delight in watching the other move into the next stage of his/her growth. If that growth takes a loved one away, then so be it. For in a PI-based view, there is no loss, since there is no possession in the first place.

The CI-based view of love, popularized in song, movies and the like, is a love of "crushing to the chest." We are told that we own and hold onto the one desired and loved, that this other person will make us whole and happy. So we are to "cage" each other for our mutual completion. We are told that to lose this love is tragic, that it may never happen again. The real tragedy is that we believe this to be true. For when we make someone into a possessed object, we have begun to kill each other. Of course, I don't mean physical homicide (though that sometimes happens), but we do kill each other mentally, by freezing expectation through conceptualization. When we buy into the idea that someone out there will love me and keep me and own me, we sacrifice the opportunity to continue our internal growth. When we place value on the quantity of time we have with someone, rather than the quality of the relationship, we sacrifice potential growth and development.

In a PI-based view we come together in a loving way to help, nurture and provide safety for our mutual growth. We do not help, nurture and provide safety for the purpose of present and future ownership. The one we love is not a share of stock that we hope will increase in value so, as owners, we can grow rich. All good parents know that child rearing is a combination of nurture and the push toward responsible independence and continued growth. The child leaves home, but that does not mean a loss to the parents. A lover or spouse leaves, and that does not mean a loss either. If higher love is present in the parting, there is joy in watching the departure when it promises new growth and learning.

People operating from the CI-based view find the idea of joyful parting difficult to understand. Messages from this idea of the world urge us to keep, have, hold. But we have seen through the history of humankind that the greatest loves are those that free us to seek our own potential and awakening. There has never been a great love that holds, possesses and binds anyone to a life of attachment and stagnation. We are all capable of exercising this great love for others and for ourselves.

MAKING THE SHIFT TO PI

SOME SAY THAT LIVING according to a PI-based view is too difficult for the ordinary person, but I reply that it is only difficult if one's attachment to the CI-based view is too strong. The strength of that attachment, curiously enough, derives not from positive attraction, but from fear. Once we let go of the fear and relax our grip on the CI-based view, the transition can begin rather smoothly, without much effort. Letting go of fear requires only that we observe it in action. When we look at it openly, that is, see it as it actually operates, without reacting to it, the fear will diminish in its strength and power to prevent the shift to PI.

The human situation is like a factory in some ways. We are usually unaware of the amount and magnitude of disorder in our lives. We simply react to the various crises that come our way, crises that derive from the normal workings of our CI-based mindset. Our desire to get and hold onto, are always going to be thwarted in the everyday world. Each time we react to changes, we waste energy trying to possess that which is impossible to retain. Watching how we react reveals to us the level of our current capability to work effectively. It soon becomes obvious that we need to let go of many impossible messages that tell us we have to control our world in a certain way, or possess our loved ones, or insist that our opinions must be right and followed by everyone.

In PI we begin to put order into our relationships with others. Order is based on consistent support and nurturance that accepts ourselves and the ones we care for. We no longer have to have our way at the expense of others. Just as the factory must first be cleaned up, with things put in their proper location and order, we begin by cleaning up our minds and placing concepts and ideas in their proper order. This internal orderliness lets us observe more clearly the way we relate to others without all the messy reactiveness of the CI-based way. We then have more energy left over to hear others and see the situation they are in, without any need to "fix" them or judge them as bad and wrong. If there is an opportunity to help, that will be obvious. If not, then we can get on with our living without carrying all the baggage of other people's issues.

This way of perceiving, thinking and acting is not cold and standoffish; quite the contrary. It is a way of deep caring, but does not take responsibility for others' living. Those in the CI-based view think that they are helping when they carry other people's burdens and take other's struggles to be their own. I find that it only colludes with the idea that we are not responsible for being who we are as humans. It is not supportive to keep people believing that someone else will come along and make their living better. Such an approach only assists others to continue in the role of victim.

When we see this process from the PI-based perspective, we simply stop colluding. There is nothing else to do. By doing nothing, things change. We change.

We are consumed by our own reactions and disorderly struggles when we continue in the CI-based way. If we do not stop, we will never see the opportunities for improvement all around us. We will pass blindly by a hundred every day and hear only our own conceptual messages about how things should be different. And things will stay the same.

ALIGNING OUR BEING

MOST OF US THINK we are a singular entity. When we say that "I decided to go to work" that we mean that with all of our being. The simple fact is that we have many internal "I"s within us and whoever happens to be operating at that moment fully believes that the decision is being made is one done by my complete self. It is only a fragment of us speaking. Within us, we have accumulated many different entities that I call the "I"s of our being. These "I"s are our images, our ego states, our roles, our identities, or other fragments of our inner system. We are many people. Our external circumstances call these various "I"s front and center. You can think of this as a stage that is within us, and our invisible director observes our immediate situation and calls the appropriate actor on stage to deal with it. When that actor "I" is on stage, it fully believes that it is the sole speaker and sole representative of our totality. This is why we can, in all sincerity, make a commitment to someone when one actor "I" is on stage and as circumstances change, can make a completely contrary commitment. It is not that we are "two faced" and liars, but that we are many faced and totally unconscious of those other parts when we are taken over by the actor "I" currently on stage. eg, The "want to be thin" I proclaims total commitment to a new eating plan and a day later, the "eating gives me pleasure" I decides to pig out on a big pizza. We do this all the time. It is simply how the system of "I"s works.

Some people think that they can go into some internal analysis and find who all these "I"s inhabiting us are and how they work. This is usually a fairly wasteful activity. First of all, the analyzer is usually another "I" within us who does not want to "see" who is in there, but wants to judge and critique them. This is what the various "I"s do. They are loaded with rules, values, concepts, scripts, and other forms of the "right way" that we have learned as we grew up. We learned some of these to protect our being, some to help us survive, and some to enhance our being. Why they came into being and what they serve is not important at this point. It is only to understand that there is whole cast of characters hiding out in you. This combination would be what most call our personality. And most of us have completely accepted this psychological explanation and just live with the hand we have dealt ourself. We created these entities for some "good" reason in our lifetime, the only question is, do we want to live in these unconscious characters any more?

If you wish to discover who you are as this array of conceptual characters, you need to apply your PI skill to observe them in action. This simply means that you begin to notice the various patterns of your reactions in the everyday situations of life. You do not judge what you see, you only observe it and, if possible, ask yourself where does that come from, what purpose does it serve, what are the messages contained in it, and how attached am I to it. No need to fix it, condemn it, or try to throw it out. When you do that, you are no longer coming from your PI place of observing. The notion of fixing, ridding, or judging can only come from another fragment of your system of "I"s. So when you do that you set up an internal war of words where one part of you wants to dominate and control another part of you. All this does is make both sides more powerful and your fragmentation more confirmed. eg, You notice that you get upset when you boss criticizes you at work and that leads to some angry and pouting behavior. Another part of you pretends to observe this activity (really judges) and says that this behavior gets you no where and isn't it best to learn from the critique and get on with work. That is your "I am competent" I speaking to the "I am a failure" I. Now as they battle, there is energy being produced by the inner chatter of both sides defending and protesting. It is this very energy that enhances and strengthens the very existence of the "I"s in the first place. This is not PI. This is judgmental analysis.

If you stay with a pure observation PI approach, the various "I"s that get called out by life's experiences will be revealed to you and by not attacking, defending or praising them, they begin to lose their energy. You just watch them play themselves out and in that playing out they are draining the energy that keeps them alive. There is nothing to do to "fix" yourself. We all tend to a healthy state when we move more to a quiet presence in the world. We can still bring some of those "I"s onto the stage in a conscious fashion if needed in certain circumstances. But we always are aware that whatever they say is only from that fragmented point of view. What you will find is that you will no longer commit to things that are contradicted by other parts of you. The other parts will hold very little say and the promises you make are made with an aligned being. You will have a different kind of energy since little will be lost to the internal battles. But at the same time, there will not be the energy that some call "motivation". ie, If your "I" to succeed and become important has lost its energy because you have observed it and let it dissipate, then that energy will not be there to take on some project that would feed that ego state. It does not mean that you become a lazy slug, if that is what you are thinking. It does mean that you have a very deep source of energy that is not torn apart to feed our internal fragmented "I"s. It can be focused like a laser when it is necessary, but when there is nothing in particular to do, it goes just as quiet as it was intense.

Lao Tzu called this the energy the "well that is never drained. This new energy is not the stored up energy of those different parts of our inner being, but an energy that comes through us, but does not belong to us. It is a constant energy that is universal. The more we stay with our Perceptual Intelligence of presence the more this energy is available to us. And of course, there is no personal gain that can be had with it. It is from the universe and it is for the universe. It is open and available to all of us, if we simply go quiet.

REFLECTIONS ON LIVING IN QUALITY

THE FOLLOWING "REFLECTIONS" WERE WRITTEN over twenty years ago, and represent my own awakening into PI. Reflection is actually a misnomer, because they came <u>through</u> me. I found myself writing automatically while the words flowed, as it were, directly to my pen. I have preserved these writings exactly as they came to me at the time. They may appear unfinished and disorganized, but I wanted to honor the source.

QUALITY OF LIVING

The quality of my living is totally dependent on the amount of <u>attention</u> I place on the process of my being.

I am like a craftsman working on a pot or a fine automobile. When he attends to the process of making, he attains quality.

Not a quality that is compared to some idea of perfection, but quality that is best that he can attain.

When he attends elsewhere, the quality diminishes for he no longer is attaining his best. The product is no longer the best quality of his attention.

In my living, it is very much the same. When I am in attention to my process of living I am living the best I can.

This is not in comparison to how someone else may live, but only the best I can do for where and what I am.

My life quality is not attached to the quantity of things around me nor to the traditional idea of the quality of things or people around me.

I and only I determine the quality of my living since I alone control the focus of my attention.

When I attend to things or ideas or events external to me rather than the process of me experiencing these things, I diminish my quality of living.

Humans possessed by attention to the content of their living, live lives of low quality even though they may "own" many things.

They, like the inattentive craftsman, finish the thing, get the results or get done, but miss the experience of the creative quality process.

April, 1980.

THE JOY OF LIKING

There is certain joy in liking my friends, I find it similar to the joy of a child with a toy. I explore and discover and mostly watch to see how you are and how you will be.
I give my attention as a gift of caring; with that giving I get you in return. For it is thru my attention that you exist to me. Therefore, my gift is the only thing I know that gets a return without anyone giving anything.
I give my attention to get the experience of you; you can give me your attention for the experience of me. But if you need to attend elsewhere, it is okay. For in the giving, I get.
By the way, attention is love.
1979.

LOVE BEFORE LIKE

As we go through this living, most of us believe that loving someone emanates from intense liking over time.

If we slow down to examine that, we can see several thoughts behind that description that need exploring before we conclude the accuracy of that.

First, is love something that grows over time? To me, that says that love is based on a set of conditions or values that, if met or aligned, will intensify the feeling of love.

Is love a meeting of conditions? Whose conditions? That seems to be more a description of like. Who do I like based on an evaluation of criteria (values and conditions) that I choose from.

Then what is love? Love is a state of being where an individual is capable of intense direct experience of another with no evaluation or conditions impinging on the interaction. That is – to totally *be* with another.

When does time then come into play? Love is timeless, since it is connected to the here and now moment and does not mean anything in past or future terms. Love is direct interaction, not a thought of the past or future.

Like can grow with time – so can dislike! As we change and grow, our sense of what is important evolves. What we use to judge like and dislike and therefore how to spend our time changes.

Now when we put these together, we can see that the best way to gather data on an individual is to totally experience them as they happen (love).

Once you have the data, you can choose to like or dislike the person when you are *not* experiencing them. Not while you *are* experiencing them.

To conclude like or dislike while experiencing puts your own thoughts in front of the actual person. All you see then is your own thoughts.

Over time, you can choose to be with someone or not. When you choose to be with someone, why not *be* with them.

Love is on their time, like is on your own time. If you never love, you don't know what you're talking about.

October 18, 1982

UNDERSTANDING AND AGREEMENT

- To understand is to agree. To not agree is to not have complete understanding. You can't understand and disagree.
- If you are disagreeing with that thought, you need to explore your understanding.
- Understanding = agreement. Agreement = understanding. We cannot have language work any other way.
- If we agree on the symbolic word "cup" to represent a cup thing, and we both agree to that, then when I say "cup", you understand our agreement and respond.
- Each word we use must be based on the same premise or we can't understand each other. This is also true with words for abstractions.
- The real difference in my living process that this realization brings is the difference in the focus of my attention and height of my awareness.
- To focus on understanding creates in me a curiosity of what is happening. Seeking understanding in process demands my careful attention to events and heightened awareness of my interaction.
- To focus on agreement creates in me a defense of my ego beliefs, values, and prior conclusions. My attention is focused internally and my awareness of interaction fades away.
- To constantly seek understanding keeps me alive and alert. There are no conclusions in understanding.
- To see agreement bounds me in my past and closes me to the world evolving in front of me.

> September 3, 1981.

USING THE MIND/BRAIN

How do we best use our mind in a way that can fully realize the capacity of our brain? This is the question of quality thinking.

First, we must be clear that the mind is that part of us that allows us to experience and have consciousness. It is our awareness.

The brain on the other hand is the storage area of all our thoughts, symbols, words, concepts, beliefs, etc. It is the integrator and assembler of thought.

With this concept in place, we need to look at how we best interact between these two entities. Most of the time this interaction is going on unconsciously.

Our best use of mind/brain would be determined by how well we can bring to bear our knowledge (stored in the brain) on the situation at hand (experienced through the mind). The quality of that use is obviously determined by the capacity of both pieces of that interaction.

We can see this clearly in other physical aspects of ourselves. We learn a sport well by practicing, and then we achieve quality on the playing field when we learn how to play reactively. In other words, without <u>thinking</u> about it.

The same is true about the intellectual side of ourselves. We must exercise the brain with concepts, ideas, etc. while we are away from the situation. We essentially are building the muscle of the brain.

The trick is to be able to suspend thinking in the real time situation so our awareness is not cluttered with our internal dialogue. Then our awareness is keen and we <u>let</u> the brain formulate the right intellectual responses. We get out of our intellect's way.

Therefore, quality of thought is that combination of a well-exercised brain given its free movement in light of the calm awareness of heightened consciousness.

February 19, 1982.

MAGIC

What is the magic of being alive? Is there such a magic?

Magic is the sense of reality of something happening that is inexplicable yet actually going on.

Inexplicable usually means in our ordinary way of describing or understanding the world. We always believe that the explanation of magic is extraordinary.

It never occurs to us that life itself is extraordinary and magic. If that is so, then there can be no explanation.

If there was no explanation (except for very small and fragmented pieces) of an alive reality, where would that leave us?

How would you look at life without explanation? What would you see? Would it all be out of control?

Think of how you look upon the magician, who before your eyes does the impossible. How is your attention? How is your focus?

Do you again capture the child in you and again discover amazement? Are you sensing your aliveness and alertness?

And, after all of that and the trick is complete and we walk away amazed and still not knowing, isn't it okay?

Isn't it okay to be ignorant and alive? Isn't it okay to not know and still witness? Isn't it okay to simply have been attentive without an answer?

The magic of life is without explanation, but it can be seen with the attentive/alert eyes of the child in us.

The seeing creates the magic and the magic creates the seeing. They are reflections.

To start the cycle, you only need to let go of the need for explanation. The magic emerges.

September 16, 1981.

PEACE

Have you ever examined what peace really is? Often used, but I see little understanding.

In the world of nature, we usually see peace as the absence of disruption. A placid scene where the weather is calm, and the animals and plants are in harmony.

In society, we see peace as the absence of war, hatred, crime, or other social disruption. There is a normal "going about business" aspect to it.

In our home, we see peace as an absence of noise, confusion, strife, etc. There is a soft lull in the usual busyness of maintaining a household.

In our head, peace is experienced as an absence of worry, concerns, fears, confusion, etc. There is the mere paying attention to the sights, sounds, and impressions of all that surrounds you.

In all of these, there is the one thing in common, and that is the absence of things. This says that in absence, the universe returns to its natural state of peace, whether it is in nature, the society, the home, or the mind.

Out of this sense of nothing comes the natural living out of things. The disruptions are all ways to shorten the natural life of things.

In nature, there are disruptors that shorten the life of one part to add to the life of others. Mankind as nature does the same.

In the realm of our consciousness, we disrupt one part to do the same. The problem is that both parts are of the same whole, therefore it must be an overall loss with no peace.

Seeking peace is to seek the absence of things to disrupt. Seeking is disruptive. Again the paradox.

Peace comes from the non-action of disrupting things. In peace, the mind/consciousness grows to its natural extent. In peace you can see the movement of the natural order of things.

January 7, 1982.

CHANGE

Change is a process of moving from one state of being to another. That applies to people and things.

Change is clear around physical things. We can see it in one state and put it through a process and then can see the changed state.

Even our bodies respond this way. We always can see a before and after appearance to the process.

Does this apply to psychological change? To really see this, one must look at those key elements of a change process.

The two key elements are duality and time. The before that changes over time to the after. This is the essence of change.

In our mind, we have tried to simulate this process in order to control and understand ourselves. We think that over time we can change from how we are to how we need or want to be.

What we need to explore is whether there needs to be a before/after or me/not-me duality and also whether or not time exists psychologically. These two are interdependent.

Duality exists over time, and time exists in duality. Before/after is connected to past/future.

So, is there really such a thing as time in our consciousness that allows for the creation of duality?

Do we always "think" in a before/after way, or can we experience the process of thought only as a moving singular point with not time associated with it?

I am not talking about what we think about. This is about the very act of thinking.

To directly experience our very act of thinking is to be in touch with the non-dual world of being fully conscious.

From this point of consciousness, time and duality fall away of themselves. We do not try to become one and timeless, it becomes us.

In this mode, we can clearly see the connectedness of the yin/yang of the physical world. We also see clearly the way we have established duality inside our mind.

The constant conflict is having one self image and trying to change what we currently think we are to that image.

We see clearly that we think there is a past that is responsible for our life now. We see clearly how we think there is a future to go to.

Once you see these, then you can decide to hold on to them or not. If we can't clearly see them, we cannot choose. Without choice, we can only believe there is no other way to be.

March 10, 1982.

ON TIME

The earth moves, the moon moves, the sun and stars shine, and man invented time.

Time is a measurement of movement from points in the past.

For physical needs, time is a useful tool to keep order and understanding.

Time does not exist psychologically.

What we call time in our heads is really memory and fantasy created by our thinking.

Memory is that psychological ability to go "back in time" and recreate in our head the experience we once had.

For physical matters that is fine; for psychological matters that blocks the ability to experience the new and present.

Fantasy is usually the projection of memory in the "future time."

We pick out of our memory the parts that would create the fantasy we have of our future.

In the physical sense, we use that to make things. Psychologically, we use that to try to capture the past, to pretend security and avoid the present.

Consciousness exists only in the present. There is no time in the immediate now. Now can't be measured since it is a singular moving point.

To think we have time (past or future) is to avoid looking at the now.

Time does not heal our pain. We do.

Things won't change with time. Things just change.

We don't have time to become anything else. We only have now.

n.d.

THE STRUGGLE – THE SACRIFICE

We are all in our unique struggle to be who we wish to be. To find the self in us who is "really" us.

We struggle with our inadequacy to live up to, to be strong, to be together, to be all that we think we ought to be.

The struggle is also in our relating to the others in our world. We struggle to be simply us amidst the demand and desires for us to become another's source of satisfaction.

The sacrifice is the ability to let go of the ego that keeps us in the struggle. The ego makes the demands like those "others."

The sacrifice is not to get our way and it's okay. The sacrifice is not to be right, and it's okay. The sacrifice is to never get there, and it's okay.

After all the sacrifice is done – the struggle changes – but does not cease.

The struggle becomes one of choosing to "be" in the responsible and connected way.

The struggle is to stay in the unitive now while feeling so much pulling from so many pieces and parts.

The struggle goes on to see ourselves unconditionally. That is, to see without comparing – without judging.

That ability to finally see ourself as an ongoing event happening in and to the world, and as we see ourselves to see the joy in that being.

At that point, the possibility of sacrifice of all that we know can lead us to all the unknown.

October 11, 1982.

FINISHING

If it be done, let it be done – for I have lived. What does that mean? I have loved and been loved. I have cared and been cared for. I have seen as it is and been seen as I am. There is no more and no less.

My heart, at times, bursts with the joy and sadness of my living. The joy of having discovered my life in a very full manner, the sadness of seeing clearly the pain of others and knowing I am helpless at making their life different. The sadness of seeing what we are doing to ourselves and others for the sake of words and ideas. At the same time, the joy of seeing the uniqueness and wonder and amazement of everyone and me.

I am surely passing through on a journey of living. Passing through this moment – not passing through from somewhere to somewhere. It's an endless journey that is also beginningless.

If it be done, let it be. The sense of finishedness stays with me and as a vague yet comfortable feeling. I could ask for no more than for what I have and am. What I have is an awareness of love in happening. I have touched people and they have touched me. I have been and be. And I am aware of that. I have shared all of me as I could. I have been shared with by others. I have seen my heart. Others have shown me theirs. I have given my heart and have been given in return. I have looked at me without condition and been able to look on others without condition. I has all come back in so many ways.

I wish to give away the secret that is no secret. All is as it should be, therefore, it is all okay to watch and be with it all. All of me, all of you, is done as we need be. Watching that evolve – transforms it.

If it be done, let it be.

September, 1979.

OTHER READINGS THAT MAY BE HELPFUL:

ALL BOOKS BY J. Krisnamurti, especially "Freedom from the Known". The series of books by Carlos Castanada, especially "Tales of Power". "Awareness" by Anthony DiMello. Various books on Zen, especially by Thomas Merton. "The Tao Te Ching" by Lao Tzu. "Power versus Force" by Hawkins. The later books by Alan Watts. "Illusions" by Richard Bach. Various books about or by Gurjieff, Ouspensky, and Bennett based on the initial work of Gurjeiff. (These are pretty difficult reading) "The Crack in the Cosmic Egg" by Pearce. There are many more out there, but the only caution is to avoid books that give answers, shoulds, values, or any set of beliefs or practices that need to be followed. They are stuck in CI. Tom Lane

ABOUT THE AUTHOR

TOM LANE has been an organizational consultant for over 30 years, focusing on the leadership of fundamental change. He is retired now and lives in Columbus, Indiana.

OTHER BOOKS BY TOM LANE
The Way of Quality
The Silent Self

CPSIA information can be obtained
at www.ICGtesting.com
Printed in the USA
FSHW010704010520
69802FS